Participant Workbook

LEGACY
Leadership
INSTITUTE

ISBN #978-0-9801965-7-3

CoachWorks® International Corporation
Dallas, Texas
www.CoachWorks.com
www.LegacyLeadership.com
info@coachworks.com

The Principals, Authors of Legacy Leadership®

Dr. Jeannine Sandstrom
Dr. Sandstrom has been a business owner and international leader coach since 1979. She has focused her leader development coaching in the practical arena of behavioral contracting, outcome clarification, and strategies to sustain performance excellence. In her 25 years of individual and organizational consulting, Jeannine coached numerous executive leaders and their teams in the high tech, communications, financial and energy industries. Sandstrom has co-authored coaching materials used extensively throughout the executive coaching industry. She has been featured on PBS specials, in The Wall street Journal and Fortune Magazine. Sandstrom holds certifications as Master Coach and Corporate Business Coach. Her doctorate is in Human Resource Development, and she holds masters degrees in Business Administration and Adult Learning.

Dr. Lee Smith
Dr. Smith is an Executive Leader Coach who has authored numerous leader coaching programs and established standards and ethics for the executive coaching profession. Smith is highly skilled in identifying key relational patterns and hidden systems that prevent groups of people from being the best they can be. As barriers are removed, she coaches and guides leaders to reorganize around successful business strategies and to establish new patterns and systems that sustain progress. Dr. Smith regularly presents at national and international professional conferences and has been featured in Newsweek, PBS Specials, and other media. Smith is one of the first internationally credentialed Master Coaches. Her Ph.D. is in Organizational Behavior and Psychology.

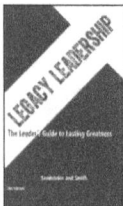

ALSO AVAILABLE: "LEGACY LEADERSHIP: The Leader's Guide to Lasting Greatness" (2nd Edition) and the "Legacy Leadership Application Workbook" by Dr. Jeannine Sandstrom and Dr. Lee Smith, authors of Legacy Leadership. Available through amazon.com and Barnes & Noble online booksellers.

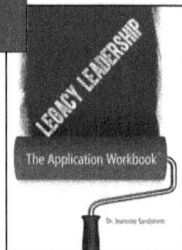

Welcome to the Legacy Leadership® Institute.

This book contains <u>three separate documents,</u> all used during the Institute, and combined into this workbook for easy use. These documents are presented in this order:

1. The Learning Journal
2. The Field Guide *(page edges marked in gray for easy reference)*
3. The Legacy Leadership Competency Inventory (LLCI)

A **Master Table of Contents** is included in the front of this Participant Workbook. It includes listings and master page numbers for each of the above documents. Page numbers run consecutively for the entire workbook.

All of these documents are referenced and used in the standard Legacy Leadership® Institute. In addition, a full color rendition of the Legacy Leadership® Model is presented on the back cover of this book.

Because of the stand-alone nature of each of these documents included in this workbook, there may be some duplication of material, but we have taken steps to avoid this wherever possible. This master workbook is designed to be used by a facilitator who will guide your use and progress through this workbook.

LEGACY
Leadership

INSTITUTE

Workbook Master Table of Contents

(continued next page...)

Workbook Master Table of Contents

Workbook Master Table of Contents

(continued)

Learning Journal

LEGACY Leadership

NAME:

About Legacy Leadership®

Welcome to the Learning Journal and Legacy Leadership®

This **Learning Journal** is the place where participants jot notes, do exercises and homework, and journal their reflections during the Legacy Leadership® Institute. Your facilitator will provide the instructions you need. You will be doing the "work" of the Institute in this Journal. Facilitator <u>may</u> include various other materials which he/she will direct you to include in proper page location.

The **Learning Journal** is designed to be used in tandem with the Legacy Leadership® **Field Guide** throughout the Institute. The bulk of actual content regarding the Legacy Leadership® Models and concepts is found in the Field Guide. Reference will be made often to the Field Guide during the Institute.

We hope that this Learning Journal will assist you in becoming a true **student of leadership**, and a *Legacy Leader®*.

Legacy Leadership® is the wisdom of the ages structured and packaged for today's - and tomorrow's - leaders.

Its truths and Best Practices are timeless, proven keys to sustained significance—and form the foundation for real-time legacy in today's business environment. No gimmicks. This is the real thing.

This unique and highly interactive learning institute will equip you with both the blueprint and the tools for a sustainable environment—all you need to build today and tomorrow for yourself, your people, and your organization. Legacy Leadership® is a complete program—a philosophy, a process, and a model. **Legacy Leadership® is not a leadership style—it is a LifeSystem.**

This vital, highly adaptable, and proven model was developed as the result of over forty years of the combined experiences of the CoachWorks® principals in individual, corporate, and organizational leadership development. CoachWorks® International has always been a thought leader, bringing innovative programs and materials to the leadership development industry. Legacy Leadership, however, is more than a program. Founders of CoachWorks® International, Drs. Smith and Sandstrom have **refined reliable time-honored principles into an intentional, powerful system for success— today and tomorrow.** For you and for others.

(continued…)

About Legacy Leadership®

Are you living your legacy? "Legacy" is commonly thought to be something you leave behind when you're gone. What if you were living your legacy now? What if your vision for the future was evident in everything you do, every day? **It can happen.**

CoachWorks® International has isolated, defined, and made transferable the practices common to leaders who are able to achieve and sustain success—**with people, product, and revenue.** Legacy Leadership® is based on 5 Best Practices which are common in all great leaders, whether it be the ancients whose successes leap from the worn pages of history, or the Fortune 500 leaders of today—and will be observed in the leaders of tomorrow.

During the Institute you will:

- **Experience a life-changing learning adventure.**

- **Become a student of leadership.**

- **Learn the basics and principles of The 5 Best Practices.**

- **Learn how to design and implement action plans to measure and grow Legacy Leadership® competencies in personal or organizational environments.**

- **Learn to utilize the components of Legacy Leadership® to set direction and achieve business results.**

- **Learn to use the Legacy Leadership® tools to bring out your best, and the best in others.**

- **Come away inspired, humbled, empowered, and alive with possibility.**

Legacy Leadership® is a philosophy, a model, and a proven process for bringing out your best, developing other leaders in your organization, and positively impacting the bottom line.

Current leader books and articles cover various aspects and techniques of leadership, but do not deliver a comprehensive model. Legacy Leadership® is a complete framework of practices, behaviors, attitudes and values that addresses every aspect of successful leadership.

You will become a student of leadership while focusing on building other leaders who build leaders, who build leaders...

CoachWorks® International

> *"In my 22 years of management consulting, Legacy Leadership® provides the most comprehensive model of what leadership is really about that I've seen. Its power in diagnosis and improvement is much greater than other models that focus only on leader behavior."*
>
> Dr. Jerry Fletcher
> Author of PATTERNS OF HIGH PERFORMANCE

Section 1

- Welcome
- Symbols of Your Leadership Style
- Leadership Learning Partners
- Leader Partner Feedback
- Leadership Challenges
- What do you want from the Course?
- Introduction of Materials
- Learning Objectives
- Leader Shifts
- What do Leaders— Know - Believe - Do
- Leaders as Expert/Mentor/Manager/Coach
- YOU Inc. & LLCI
- Legacy Leadership® Model
- Your BP Focus
- Reflections

Leader Partner Introduction Sheet

Leader Name: _____

Business: _____

_____

Personal Objective for this Institute: _____

_____

_____

_____

Something fun and/or unusual about you that no one would guess: _____

_____

_____

_____

Leader Partner Feedback

Observe your Leader Partner being a Legacy Leader®. Record your feedback here and hold until Day 3 when you will coach your partner around your observations.

You were effective when you...	The positive impact to the team was...	This was a great example of Legacy Leadership® Best Practice:				
		1	2	3	4	5

1—Holder of Vision and Values™
2—Creator of Collaboration and Innovation™
3—Influencer of Inspiration and Leadership™
4—Advocator of Differences and Community™
5—Calibrator of Responsibility and Accountability™

Institute Objectives

Learning Objectives

Upon completion of this Institute program the participant will be able to:

☐ **Learning Objective 1**
Describe for others the Business Case for integrating Legacy Leadership® into the fabric of all interactions and offerings.

☐ **Learning Objective 2**
Identify and practice teaching the key competencies and behaviors associated with each of the 5 Best Practices.

☐ **Learning Objective 3**
Demonstrate the use of the LL Competency Inventory (LLCI) as a tool to aid others in developing competencies in other leaders.

☐ **Learning Objective 4**
Explain his or her own concrete action plan to inspire, equip, gain commitment for and grow Legacy Leader® in all walks of life.

☐ **Learning Objective 5**
List the linkages between LL principles and positive business results to create the business application for LL in the marketplace.

The Ideal Leader

What constitutes the INFLUENTIAL LEADER?

What does the IDEAL LEADER.....		
KNOW?	BELIEVE?	DO?

Benchmark Your Leadership

Who are you as a Leader?

Rating Key:

5=Consistently
4=Frequently
3=On Average
2=Occasionally
1=Not at All

#	Question	Rate Yourself 1-5
1.	I link new initiatives with the organization's strategic vision.	
2.	My values are consistently demonstrated in the decisions I make.	
3.	I am known as an innovator who gets things done.	
4.	I set the tone for collaboration rather than competition.	
5.	I mentor others by focusing on their accomplishments.	
6.	I pay attention to the best way of developing others.	
7.	I am able to match the right people with the right job for them and the organization.	
8.	I value the uniqueness of each person on my team.	
9.	I provide clear benchmarks and milestones for achieving goals.	
10.	I define clear accountabilities for my team and myself and follow up consistently.	
	Total Points	

Interpreting Leadership Levels of Practice

Aware:	10-15
Knowledgeable:	16-24
Apprentice:	25-39
Proficient:	40-45
Master:	46-50

Legacy of Leadership

What Legacy are you living?

Step 1: Think of yourself as 'You Inc.'. With you at the top (or in the middle) of your organizational chart, identify all the people you are in relationship with. This includes work, home, community, church, sports etc.

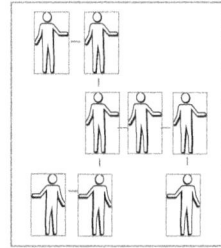

Name names...

Step 2: In a second level of consideration, identify who the first level are in relationship with. Name names...

The Model

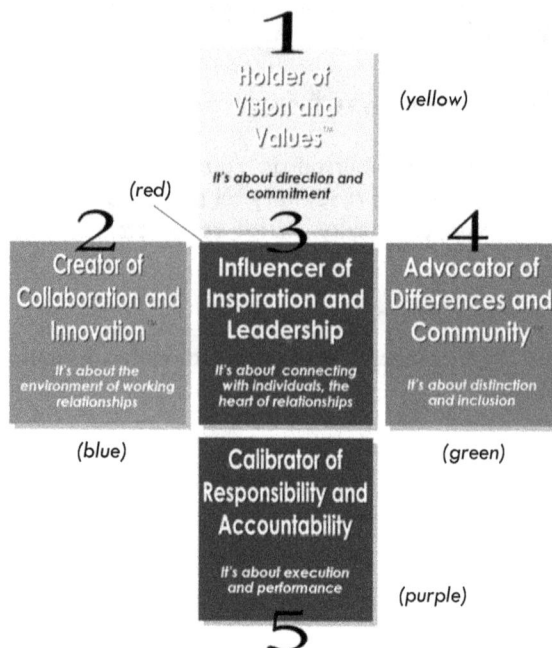

We are often asked about the colors used in the Legacy Leadership® logo and model. Do they have significance? We wanted bright, bold, crisp and clean colors for this leadership model—well defined, highly visible and not muted—just like our leadership and our legacy should be. That was the primary motivator for selecting the colors found here. The colors were also identified with each of the 5 Best Practices in order to provide some easily remembered association.

Yellow, bright and "sunny," is often associated with light and vision. **Yellow is the color of Best Practice 1: Holder of Vision and Values**™. The Legacy Leader® holds and sustains the vision, aligning it with values (personally, professionally, and organizationally). Without this "light," goals remain in the dark. The Legacy Leader® carries the light of vision everywhere. This Best Practice is about direction and commitment.

Blue is the color of cloudless skies. It reminds us of great expanses, unlimited horizons and rich opportunities. For this reason, **blue has been assigned to Best Practice 2: Creator of Collaboration and Innovation**™. A creator brings something into being through original and inventive means. A Legacy Leader® creates collaboration and innovation, painting a wide and limitless picture of new possibilities—the sky is the limit. This Best Practice is about creating a positive environment for working relationships.

Red is the color of the heart. It is associated with the very core and being of something, and thus it has been **linked with Best Practice 3: Influencer of Inspiration and Leadership**™. This Best Practice is the heart of Legacy Leadership®. The Legacy Leader® influences, inspires and models excellence in leadership for everyone. This Best Practice is about making connections with individuals—the heart of relationships as well as leadership.

Green is the color of growth. Personal, professional and organizational growth is stimulated by drawing upon the strengths of others, which is the intent of **Best Practice 4: Advocate of Differences and Community**™. The Legacy Leader® intentionally recognizes differences as potential strengths and community growth stimulators. This Best Practice is about distinguishing individual strengths and inclusion of differing perspectives into one community.

Purple is a color often associated with royalty, and royalty can imply authority—and accountability. A king's subjects are called upon to give account for their service under him. They are responsible to him. **Purple has been assigned to Best Practice 5: Calibrator of Responsibility and Accountability**™. We believe this is a noble Best Practice, and one most often misunderstood and neglected! This Best Practice is about execution and performance measured against vision and values.

NOTE: A full color rendition of the Legacy Leadership Model is found on the back cover of this book.

Homework

Section 1 Homework/Fieldwork

Read through the **Business Applications for Legacy Leadership in the Resources Section.** Highlight the entries that had the greatest meaning for you. How would you utilize any of this material to make a case for Legacy Leadership® to individuals, or to your organization? Use this page to write down any thoughts you have during your review of these materials, and how you can make the information specific to your situation. ***Homework/Fieldwork will be debriefed and discussed before Section 2.***

Teachback Notes

Use this page to EITHER prepare for your teachback (if you have volunteered to do this) OR to record your notes from the teachback presented by other participants.

Section 2
BP 1
BP 5
BP 3

- Team Presentations
- (Review)
- BP 1 - Overview/Definitions
- Values Identifications
- Vision Creations
- BP 5 - Overview/Definitions
- Mapping Your Plan
- BP 3 - Overview/Definitions
- Qualities of Inspirational Leaders
- Story Telling
- Reflections

THE ESSENCE

Leaders embody, hold out for all to know, company's vision and values. Vision and values spell out where a company is going and the guiding principles by which they will operate. Leaders' behaviors are such that all work is organized around these 2 factors and leadership team, all performance measured against them.

Best Practice 1: **HOLDER OF VISION AND VALUES™**
BEING: Holder
Great leaders are conscious guardians of both personal and organizational vision and values. It becomes part of who they are, and guides all they do. BEING a Holder implies understanding the necessity of never allowing vision and values to slip out of focus or priority. Merely having vision, or having values is not enough. They must be intentionally held. A Legacy Leader® is very clear about his or her own personal core vision and values, which are the driving forces for their leadership. Leadership is not just about doing vision, and doing values—professionally or organizationally. A Legacy Leader® LIVES them, preserves them, and relies upon them as a guide.

BP1

Defining the Terms

Best Practice 1: Holder of Vision and Values™		
	Your PERSONAL Definition of These Words	Further understanding of these words:
HOLDER (The "Being")		
VISION		
VALUES		

Comments

BP1

A HOLDER "keeps in hand" those things that are important, embracing and encouraging their remembrance.

VISION

VISION is a clear view and understanding of realizable goals, plans and intentions

Behaviors and Competencies that distinguish a Holder of Vision

1. Clearly understands, aligns around, makes decisions that support and defend the organizational vision.
2. Integrates the vision into all responsibilities.
3. Teams translate and align with organization's vision in its daily responsibilities for meeting the goals of the organization.
4. Has a well-defined strategic plan for accomplishing goals of the vision.
5. Establishes measurable milestones and benchmarks congruent with the vision.
6. Provides consistent focus and direction.
7. Makes vision come alive in everyday activities.

VALUES

VALUES are those things considered right, worthwhile, and desirable – the basis of guiding principles and standards.

Behaviors and Competencies that distinguish a Holder of Values

1. Has a set of clearly defined personal values, standards and guiding principles.
2. Ensures that the values are integrated into how business is done.
3. "Walks the talk" and models values-based behavior.
4. Does not cover up mistakes or compromise values.
5. Decisions are made based on a core set of values.
6. Protects personal and organizational values from becoming eroded.
7. Models authenticity—personal and professional life is seamless.
8. Encourages values-driven achievement in others.

ESSENCE OF BEST PRACTICE 1

1. Effectively communicates and sustains processes to achieve the vision and uphold the values throughout the business area of responsibility.

2. Has a strong value of developing others.

When your Facilitator assigns you a few of the competencies listed to the left, circle them. Provide notes regarding a "How To" guide to accomplish these points. You may use any of the materials given you to help in this exercise. Draw on your own experiences. Try to provide practical guidelines for how these competencies can be modeled in the workplace. You will be reporting back your "How To's" to the group. You may present your information in any method you choose (teach, do a skit, tell a story, sing a song—it's your choice!)

BP1

Important Pieces

Best Practice 1 is only successful if the key pieces are in place. Using the list on the previous page select, according to your understanding of this BP, what you consider to be the 7 most important pieces (behaviors) that TOGETHER make the whole picture of BP 1. Label the puzzle pieces below with the 7 behaviors you believe are the most important. Write down any thoughts about these, and be prepared to discuss your answers.

Comments

BP 1

Developing Personal Vision

Write Your Personal Vision Statement

Vision means you have an inner calling, something within that needs to be intentionally identified and stated. It defines how we combine our strengths, our needs and our intentions with enjoyable and fulfilling pursuits. A very brief example of a personal vision statement is "To serve as a catalyst revolutionizing the lives of individuals and their companies." Generally, a personal vision statement will actually include several statements that, taken together, become a singular statement about that person's goals, aims, ambitions, capabilities, beliefs, and desires. To be representative of the person, however, it must be written with all their strengths, needs and intentions in mind.

Developing this personal vision statement requires thoughtful reflection. Consider the following as you develop your statement:

- **The big picture of your life**
- **The things you find most enjoyable**
- **Your strengths**
- **Your needs**
- **Your intentions for life**
- **Your life goals**
- **Your career goals**
- **Where you find significance, fulfillment, passion**
- **Your internal wants and desires (other than material things)**
- **Your wants for others**
- **Your values and beliefs**

After giving careful thought to the above considerations, develop a series of statements using this pattern:

- **ACTION**
  (use a verb to denote what you will DO)

- **OBJECTIVE**
  (the value or aim of the action)

- **WITH WHAT OR WHOM**
  (the thing, person, group of importance to you)

(see next page for exercise)

SAMPLE—
My vision is:

To create
  ACTION (use a verb to denote what you will DO)

positive environments
  OBJECTIVE (the value or aim of the action)

for shifts in individuals or organizations I coach.
  WITH WHAT OR WHOM (the thing, person, group of importance to you)

Vision Statement:
My vision is to create positive environments for shifts in individuals or organizations I coach.

BP1

Developing Vision

My Personal Vision Statement

If necessary, write as many statements as you need to identify your vision.

Write these statements here: **My vision is....**

1.

2.

3.

4.

5.

6.

7.

8.

9.

10.

Now here's a real challenge. Can you write a single statement that encompasses all of the above into one comprehensive personal vision statement? Think about it carefully. If you could express your entire vision in one sentence, how would you write it?

Do it here....

BP1

Developing Values

The following is excerpted from a more intensive exercise from "Developing Vision and Values" by CoachWorks International. Spend some time looking at these PERSONAL-PROFESSIONAL-SPIRITUAL values and determine which are of highest value to you. Rank them from 1 (lowest value) to 5 (highest value). Continued on next page.

#	VALUE	1	2	3	4	5	COMMENT
WHAT IS OF PERSONAL VALUE TO YOU?							
1	Knowledge of self						
2	Being "together"						
3	Congruent life in all areas						
4	Continued life education						
5	Balanced life						
6	Excellent physical health						
7	Being in control						
8	Personal development						
9	Financial wealth						
10	Positive attitude						
11	Stroked ego						
12	High self-esteem						
13	Personal grooming						
14	Serving others						
15	High energy						
16	Well educated						
17	Personal integrity						
18	Open minded/accepting						
19	Pleasant surroundings						
20	Good relationships						
21							
22							
WHAT IS OF PROFESSIONAL VALUE TO YOU?							
1	Making it to the "top"						
2	Great network						
3	Serving others						
4	Making lots of money						
5	Integrity						
6	Good working relationships						
7	Doing my best						
8	Always learning, developing						
9	Pleasant environment						
10	Being happy at work						
11	Being a leader						
12	Organization						
13	Being focused						
14	Being in control						
15	Fitting in						
16	Adaptive and flexible						
17	Being right						
18	Collaboration						
19	Ethics						
20	Acknowledgement/reward						
21							
22							

BP1

Developing Values

#	VALUE	1	2	3	4	5	COMMENT
WHAT IS OF SPIRITUAL VALUE TO YOU?							
1	Having a faith						
2	Knowing about my faith						
3	Living my faith						
4	Continued faith learning						
5	Sharing my faith						
6	Submission to my faith						
7	Being with others of my faith						
8	Understanding my faith						
9	My spiritual future						
10	Spiritual failure of others						
11	Respect for faith of others						
12	Spiritual relationships						
13	Faith-shaped values						
14	Faith values obvious in all areas of my life						
15	Faith integrity (actions match beliefs)						
16	Positive spiritual attitude						
17	Rewarding spiritual life						
18	Faith as foundation for all other activities						
19	Faith as basis for priorities						
20	Contentment with my faith						
21							
22							

Think About This...

1. Where are your "5" responses? What items listed here did you find most valuable to you? Can you comment on why this is so?

2. Did any of your responses surprise you (including your personalized fill-in blanks)? Why?

3. Do you notice any "clustering" of values? That is, certain related items all scoring high or low marks? If so, what and why? (for example, you scored 5s on items all related to sharing, or all related to contentment, or all related to self-esteem, etc.)

BP1

Developing Values

Corporate Values

As a personal or organizational exercise, begin to list (and then add as you think of more) values which you know to be those of your organization, or those you would want to be held by an organization for which you worked. Depending on your situation, you may wish to share this list with others on your team and within your organization as a tool to gain clarity and understanding around your organization's values. If you are not working within an organization at this time, you might choose to use this list as a reference guide for any organization you might serve in the future, or to help clients or others develop their own corporate values.

RANK	CORPORATE VALUE	RANK	CORPORATE VALUE

BP1

Imperatives to Remember About BP 1

BP 1 Terminal Learning Objectives

As we leave this Best Practice, scan this overview that highlights the learnings taught.

Overview

Definitions

Values Identifications

Vision Creations

Reflections

BP 1

Best Practice 5

THE ESSENCE

Leaders who demonstrate personal standards of behavior and accountability, who provide clarity about expectations for results and who ensure measurement of progress toward the vision, with an eye for flexibility and mid-course corrections.

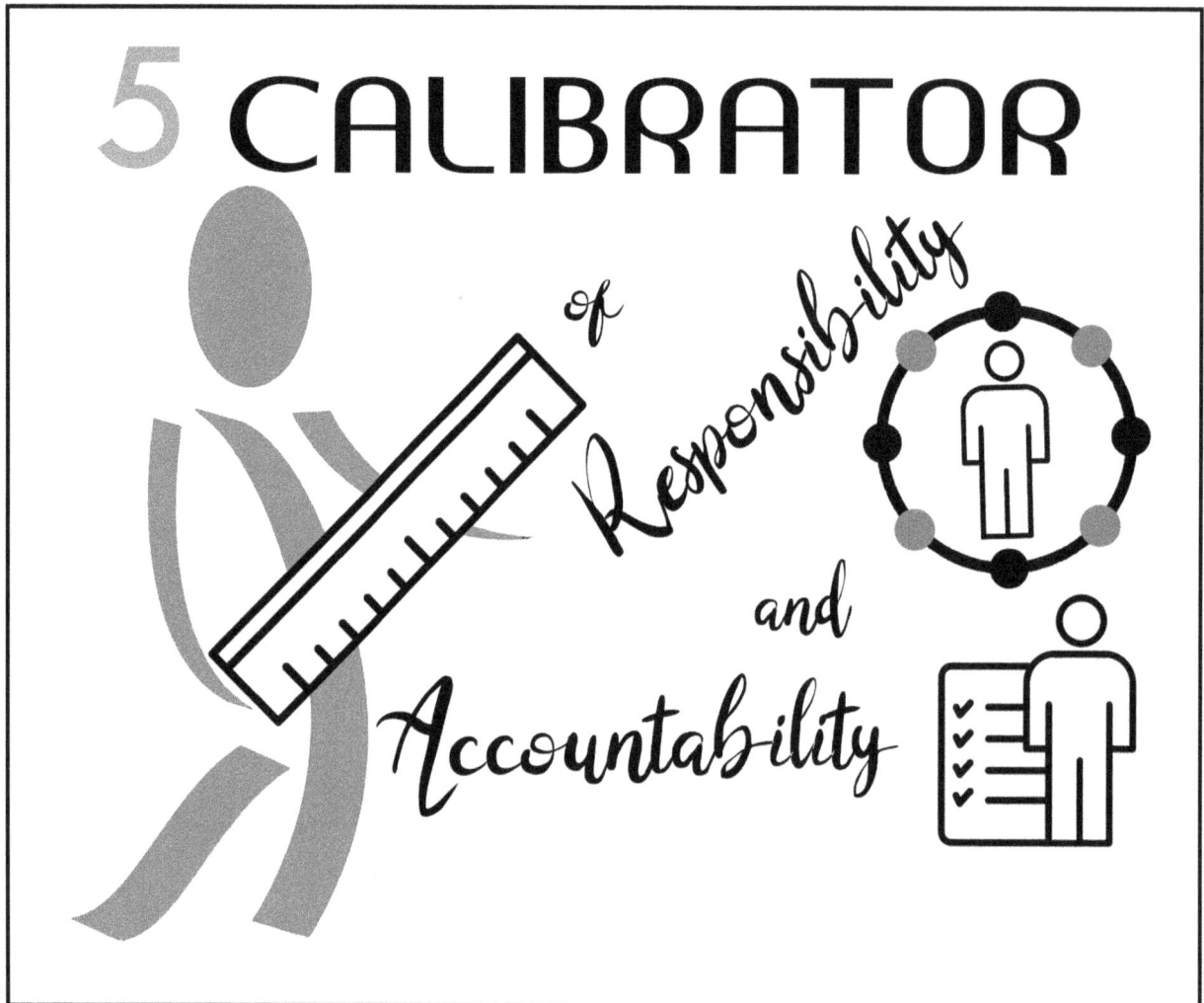

Best Practice 5: CALIBRATOR of RESPONSIBILITY and ACCOUNTABILITY™
BEING: Calibrator
A calibrator is one who is clear about standards, vision, values, and what is right both personally and organizationally, and measures all behavior against them. This is an ongoing internal process that never stops. It is a natural, conscious and continual setting of the "mark" and adjusting what is necessary to hit it consistently. It implies a sense of awareness, measurement and appropriate adjustment. Again, it is not just doing, it is being vigilant, accountable, responsible, thoughtful and nimble, with a constant eye on the target. A Legacy Leader® is a human thermostat, always measuring the environment and adjusting as necessary.

BP5

Defining the Terms

Best Practice 5: Calibrator of Responsibility and Accountability™		
	Your PERSONAL Definition of These Words	Further understanding of these words:
CALIBRATOR (The "Being")		
RESPONSIBILITY		
ACCOUNTABILITY		

Comments

BP 5

BP5: Competencies and Behaviors

A **CALIBRATOR** "sets the mark" for the quantitative measurement of success.

RESPONSIBILITY

RESPONSIBILITY is the ability to respond correctly to—and meet—stated expectations.

Behaviors and Competencies that distinguish a Calibrator of Responsibility

1. Constantly executes strategies, measuring against stated vision.
2. Has "finger on the pulse" to listen for and expect progress toward milestones and benchmarks.
3. Insures that everyone is clear about expectations.
4. Has the right people in the right positions. Requires peak performance, provides feedback/ coaching to develop it.
5. Takes appropriate and honorable action when performance does not meet expectations.
6. Knows how to celebrate successes. Focuses on what went right and what can be done differently, not what went wrong.
7. Holds self responsible first, provides a consistent role model of acceptable, expected behavior, makes no exceptions for self or others.
8. Makes perceived "failures" opportunities for learning.

ACCOUNTABILITY

ACCOUNTABILITY is the obligation to justify conduct, conditions or circumstances.

Behaviors and Competencies that distinguish a Calibrator of Accountability

1. Has clearly defined accountabilities and calibration plan for self and organization with action plan and appropriate measurables.
2. Sense of urgency both in goal accomplishment and response to change.
3. Understands this is a growth process. Provides resources so workers can learn and fulfill responsibilities.
4. Commitment follow-through with a system for promise management.
5. Regular community accountability sessions to evaluate process and outcomes.
6. Understands and communicates differences in short-term and long-term performance outcomes.
7. Keeps community of workers in partnership and ownership of overall process, and fully able and willing to be accountable together.

ESSENCE OF BEST PRACTICE 5

1. Is constantly alert to trends that may alter results and recalibrates action plans when necessary.

2. Has gained commitment from everyone in area of responsibility and accountabilities with appropriate consequences and rewards.

When your Facilitator assigns you a few of the competencies listed to the left, circle them. Provide notes regarding a "How To" guide to accomplish these points. You may use any of the materials given you to help in this exercise. Draw on your own experiences. Try to provide practical guidelines for how these competencies can be modeled in the workplace. You will be reporting back your "How To's" to the group. You may present your information in any method you choose (teach, do a skit, tell a story, sing a song—it's your choice!)

BP5

Facilitation Exercise

You and your team are now facilitators, and your Institute Facilitators are now your learners. You must, as a team, prepare to teach all you can determine about Best Practice #5—Calibrator of Responsibility and Accountability™. You may use all materials you have been given, any materials in the room available to you, and you may present in any manner or method you like, but you MUST present as a team. You only have 15 minutes to prepare, and 10 minutes to present. Use this page to write down your methods, your materials, draw pictures, doodle out your ideas, or whatever.

BP5

LEGACY LEADERSHIP® INSTITUTE PARTICIPANT WORKBOOK © 2001-2020. COACHWORKS® International. Dallas, TX USA. All Rights Reserved.
Page 37

Mapping the Plan for Organizational Results

1 Use this template for developing a case for change (e.g., justifying budget items, developing action plans, or identifying measurements and milestones).

2 LEADER SHIFTS		**3** Observable and Measurable DIFFERENCES (What will you see)
FROM	➡ **TO**	
Identify language that clearly represents the current state and desired state (before and after shift).		When you reach the desired state, what changes will you be able to observe and measure?

ACTION ITEMS (Making it happen)	**7** RESULTS (Impact on the Organization)
4 How will you bring about the desired state?	In what ways will the organization be impacted (e.g. increased earnings per share, improved retention rates)?
HOW?	
5 Who possesses the appropriate strengths for this effort?	
WHO WILL DO IT?	
6 When do you expect completion?	
PROJECTED TIMELINE	

Imperatives to Remember About BP 5

BP 5 Terminal Learning Objectives

As we leave this Best Practice, scan this overview that highlights the learnings taught.

Overview

Definitions

Mapping Your Plan

Reflections

BP5

THE ESSENCE

Leaders are "trail blazers" with a positive influence so that everyone is lifted up to be the best they can be. Participants are invited (not commanded) to contribute from strengths and are filled with energy to deliver high quality outcomes.

Best Practice 3: **INFLUENCER of INSPIRATION AND LEADERSHIP**™
BEING: Influencer
A Legacy Leader® understands that we cannot NOT influence, and therefore becomes an intentional influencer. It is about having a consciousness that all that we do influences, even when we aren't aware of it. In all we do, we will either influence in a positive or negative way. The Legacy Leader® makes a choice to BE an influencer in a positive way, regardless of the situation or circumstances. This becomes a way of life, a way of being. This awareness tempers our behavior both personally and professionally.

BP3

Defining the Terms

Best Practice 3: Influencer of Inspiration and Leadership™		
	Your PERSONAL Definition of These Words	Further understanding of these words:
INFLUENCER (The "Being")		
INSPIRATION		
LEADERSHIP		

Comments

BP3

The Influential Leader

What Does the Influential Leader Look Like?

Write down the name of the most influential person you know, or have known, and their characteristics.

BP3

An INFLUENCER brings about a desired effect in others, by direct or indirect means.

INSPIRATION

INSPIRATION is the process of animating, motivating or encouraging others to reach new levels of achievement.

Behaviors and Competencies that distinguish an Influencer of Inspiration

1. Easily builds and maintains relationships.
2. Is consistently self-inspired, and knows what inspires others.
3. Has a personal repertoire of inspirational stories. Has high level of emotional intelligence allowing ease of connection.
4. Brings out the best in people; acknowledges and recognizes their contributions.
5. Expresses a positive, powerful hope for the future - both personally and organizationally.
6. Models positive perspectives in situations.
7. Connects personally with others, valuing them individually and corporately.

LEADERSHIP

LEADERSHIP is the process of guiding and directing others to shared success.

Behaviors and Competencies that distinguish an Influencer of Leadership

1. Uses positive and uplifting language, even in crises or other challenging moments.
2. Has an excellent working knowledge of cutting edge leadership technologies, models, styles and language.
3. Provides appropriate opportunities to develop the leadership abilities, skills and styles in those they lead, and considers everyone a potential leader.
4. Invites versus commands.
5. Instills confidence.
6. Courage to take risks, make tough decisions, inspire others to follow.
7. Diffuses conflict and confrontation with positive energy.

ESSENCE OF BEST PRACTICE 3

1. Leads with great humility and focuses on people, who create the success.

2. Simultaneously, leads with fierce resolve to take the organization and the workers to greater heights of success.

When your Facilitator assigns you a few of the competencies listed to the left, circle them. Provide notes regarding a "How To" guide to accomplish these points. You may use any of the materials given you to help in this exercise. Draw on your own experiences. Try to provide practical guidelines for how these competencies can be modeled in the workplace. You will be reporting back your "How To's" to the group. You may present your information in any method you choose (teach, do a skit, tell a story, sing a song—it's your choice!)

BP3

Situational Story Development

Situational Storytelling: The influencing connection that keeps on giving!
The most impactful method of influence is through the ability to tell a persuasive story that connects both with the heart as well as the head, then translates to the hands and feet!

From   **To**

"I think I connect well with people."	"I've been told I work well with people and in my most recent positions, it was a good thing I did! I inherited a creative team that didn't get along well at all. In fact, they couldn't seem to agree on anything. So, I met with the leaders of each group to discuss their objectives, problems, and desires. Then, after I spent some time sorting out what I heard in those meetings and drew some conclusions, I brought the group leaders together and shared my conclusions. To everyone's surprise, they all agreed with me. After some nervous laughter, camaraderie started to develop and the group leaders continued to meet on a regular basis. Today, they are the smoothest operating team in the organization." *From: Lions Don't Need To Roar by D.A. Benton, 1992. Warner Books*

Components of an Inspiring Story

How To Tell a Story To Make a Connection

1. Draw from your own experiences.
2. Constantly add to your personal story collection.
3. Keep a file of stories.
4. Use descriptions.
5. Be personal.
6. Vary the length of your anecdotes and make sure any story you tell gets to its point quickly.
7. Inject humor whenever and wherever you can.

Seven Elements of Your Story

1. Introduction and setting of characters
2. Explanation of state of affairs
3. Initiating event: A situation
4. Emotional response OR statement of goal by the protagonist
5. Complicating actions
6. An outcome
7. Reactions to the outcome

For the exercise, choose one of the five Best Practices, and build a story (using the above guidelines) from your own experience to illustrate the concepts of this Best Practice. Use the lined pages to capture your story in bullet format, so you may share easily with other participants.

My story to share will illustrate:

o   Best Practice 1: Holder of Vision and Values™
o   Best Practice 2: Creator of Collaboration and Innovation™
o   Best Practice 3: Influencer of Inspiration and Leadership™
o   Best Practice 4: Advocator of Differences and Community™
o   Best Practice 5: Calibrator of Responsibility and Accountability™

BP3

Situational Storytelling Exercise

Your Story

_____

_____

_____

_____

_____

_____

_____

_____

_____

_____

_____

_____

_____

_____

_____

_____

_____

_____

_____

_____

_____

_____

_____

_____

_____

_____

_____

_____

_____

_____

_____

_____

BP3

Situational Storytelling Worksheet

Stories to Illustrate Legacy Leadership

One Story (or example) that illuminated my understanding of Legacy Leadership®:

My story to demonstrate Best Practice 1 – Holder of Vision and Values™:

My story to demonstrate Best Practice 2– Creator of Collaboration and Innovation™:

My story to demonstrate Best Practice 3– Influencer of Inspiration and Leadership™:

BP3

Situational Storytelling Worksheet

My story to demonstrate Best Practice 4—Advocator of Differences and Community™:

My story to demonstrate Best Practice 5—Calibrator of Accountability and Responsibility™:

How I will incorporate Storytelling as a powerful leadership tool:

How I will inspire other Leaders to model Storytelling as a powerful leadership tool:

BP3

Situational Storytelling Exercise

_____
_____
_____
_____
_____
_____
_____
_____
_____
_____
_____
_____
_____
_____
_____
_____
_____
_____
_____
_____
_____
_____
_____
_____
_____
_____
_____
_____
_____
_____
_____
_____
_____
_____
_____

BP3

Situational Storytelling Exercise

The Stories of Others

_____
_____
_____
_____
_____
_____
_____
_____
_____
_____
_____
_____
_____
_____
_____
_____
_____
_____
_____
_____
_____
_____
_____
_____
_____
_____
_____
_____
_____

BP3

Imperatives to Remember About BP 3

BP 3 Terminal Learning Objectives

As we leave this Best Practice, scan this overview that highlights the learnings taught.

Overview

Definitions

Qualities of Inspirational Leaders

Story Telling

Reflections

BP3

Homework

Section 2 Homework

Choose any or ALL of the following:

o   Complete the worksheets "Developing Vision" and "Developing Values" in the Resources Section of this journal. These pages are about personal vision and values.

o   Review the Field Guide content for Best Practices 1, 5, and 3, especially the Aerial Views of each.

o   Journal answers to these questions: How am I an influential leader who inspires others? How am I not? How can I improve, and what concrete steps will I take do that?

o   Use these pages to record any thoughts as you do these exercises. Homework will be debriefed in the next section.

Teachback Notes

Use this page to EITHER prepare for your teachback (if you have volunteered to do this) OR to record your notes from the teachback presented by another participant.

Section 3
BP 2
BP 4

- Team Presentations
- (Review)
- BP 2 - Overview/Definitions
- Building Trust
- BP 4 - Overview/Definitions
- PSCI
- Legacy Synthesis
- House of Legacy
- Development Plan & Review
- Institute Evaluation
- Learner Partner Symbol Exchange
- Reflections

THE ESSENCE

Leaders supply environments where team members are comfortable enough to create possibilities greater than they would have alone. The group then discovers new practices, tools or products that can changes or improve everything.

Best Practice 2: **CREATOR of COLLABORATION and INNOVATION**™
BEING: Creator

Collaboration and Innovation don't happen by themselves. They must be encouraged and nurtured, with opportunities created by leaders. This is not about being <u>creative</u>, it is about being a <u>creator</u>, one who instinctively creates opportunities where collaboration and innovation can flourish. A creator actually causes something to come into being, in this case collaboration and innovation, sometimes through inventive means. The Legacy Leader® becomes an active "opportunity seeker" and possibility thinker. This is an attitude of leadership, not just a leadership action.

BP2

Defining the Terms

Best Practice 2: Creator of Collaboration and Innovation™		
	Your PERSONAL Definition of These Words	Further understanding of these words:
CREATOR (The "Being")		
COLLABORATION		
INNOVATION		

Comments

BP2: Competencies and Behaviors

> *A CREATOR causes something to "come into being" through original or inventive means.*

COLLABORATION

COLLABORATION is the process of working together to achieve common goals instead of personal agenda.

Behaviors and Competencies that distinguish a Creator of Collaboration

1. Personally creates and fosters a learning, trusting environment.
2. Puts aside own ego to hear brilliance of others.
3. Encourages communication and openness by working to build trust.
4. Listens masterfully.
5. Asks tough questions to which answers are not known, and carefully considers the answers.
6. Speaks the truth with respect and clarity.
7. Honors differences of opinion and understands how learning occurs from disagreements.
8. Encourages everyone's participation. No holdouts! Communicates expectation of collaboration (what does it look like?).
9. Focuses on "greater good" of organization, beyond team framework.

INNOVATION

INNOVATION is the introduction of something new and different to the process of achieving goals.

Behaviors and Competencies that distinguish a Creator of Innovation

1. Sets the tone for thinking beyond the present and outside the norm.
2. Clearly establishes the process for and reaffirms value of gaining individual input.
3. Conveys that there are no bad ideas, but rather a number of options.
4. Documents and logs all ideas.
5. Can project how ideas play out in the marketplace.
6. Has a high level of personal "agility" - ability to shift thinking and performance quickly.
7. Always learning—encourages others to do so.
8. Generates excitement for shared innovation and results.

ESSENCE OF BEST PRACTICE 2

1. Is keenly aware when change needs to occur and when it does not.
2. Is a masterful facilitator of innovative thinking and conversation.

When your Facilitator assigns you a few of the competencies listed to the left, circle them. Provide notes regarding a "How To" guide to accomplish these points. You may use any of the materials given you to help in this exercise. Draw on your own experiences. Try to provide practical guidelines for how these competencies can be modeled in the workplace. You will be reporting back your "How To's" to the group. You may present your information in any method you choose (teach, do a skit, tell a story, sing a song—it's your choice!)

BP2

Building Trust That Leads to a Team's Collaborative Innovation Competencies

Legacy Leaders® establish environments that facilitate discovery of possibilities beyond conventional wisdom that taps the unique genius/gifts of all involved. The leader's job is to accept, honor, respect and facilitate each person's contributions/ideas, including options different than their own. Innovative possibilities result in leading-edge competitive positioning based on the vision and values template. This best practice fosters a "Star Wars" culture where Legacy Leaders® serve as Jedi Masters.

Successful teams must be committed to raise a standard in one area (team trust) in order to build competency in another area (creative collaboration). Review the Legacy Teams information at the right, score the index, and use the questions below to sharpen your skills.

THE TRUST INDEX

Circle the appropriate number that designates your comfort with building a "real" trust level in your team. Make sure that you are totally truthful with yourself.

SCORING PARAMETERS:
1—Not at all
2—Somewhat
3—Am able to do so
4—Do this easily
5—Insist on always doing this

#						
1	As a team member/leader, I feel responsible for creating an environment of trust where members feel comfortable speaking their truth.	1	2	3	4	5
2	I own that my truth is merely my perception and never insist that my truth is the only truth.	1	2	3	4	5
3	I know that people may disagree with my perception of the truth and believe that when disagreements occur, so does learning.	1	2	3	4	5
4	I offer my thoughts, ideas, reservations, and concerns in order that collective wisdom may be enhanced.	1	2	3	4	5
5	I feel responsible for contributing as much to the collaboration of the team as possible.	1	2	3	4	5
6	I am not afraid to speak my truth to the team.	1	2	3	4	5
7	I neither embellish nor underreport my truth.	1	2	3	4	5
8	I do not withhold information that needs to be shared with the team.	1	2	3	4	5
9	I trust that team members will not "shoot the messenger."	1	2	3	4	5
10	I accept the information offered from other members as neither wrong nor right, but as added input.	1	2	3	4	5

SCORING: Add all circled numbers and find the category that fits you.
0 to 20   Your integrity isn't showing. Work with your Coach!
20 to 40   You have average trust levels.
40 to 50   Your team/employees/customers will appreciate your integrity

Legacy Teams:

Trust each other. This means they:

- Have high standards for their interactions and communications.
- Collaborate where options and outcomes are synergistic versus individualistic.
- Respectfully give and receive feedback to each other by speaking the truth.
- Support, learn from, and encourage each other with all ideas valued.

Imagine a meeting where:

- Members look forward to attending, come prepared, participate collaboratively.
- Members collectively approach each issue from "out-of-the-box" thinking.
- Real issues are drawn out and collaboratively managed.
- The environment is a learning environment.
- Differences are honored and respected.
- Communication is clear, laser and succinct.
- Disagreement is embraced and considered a time to learn additional information.
- Clarity is alive and well.
- Interaction is fun and invigorating.
- The work of the team is done in half the time with double the results.

Consider the following:

1. Describe the best collaborative/innovative team in which you have been a member. What guiding principles had them be a committed team?

2. What ways will each of you take personal responsibility to contribute to the team trust and team collaboration?

3. How will you hold yourself and each other accountable for team collaboration?

BP2

Imperatives to Remember About BP 2

BP 2 Terminal Learning Objectives

As we leave this Best Practice, scan this overview that highlights the learnings taught.

Overview

Definitions

Building Trust

Reflections

BP 2

Best Practice 4

THE ESSENCE

Leaders possess a mindset that all people have unique and compelling contributions to make. Leaders speak up for each person to forward that person's development and progress with the company.

4 ADVOCATOR of Differences and Community

Best Practice 4: ADVOCATOR of DIFFERENCES and COMMUNITY™
BEING: Advocator
An advocator is one who stands firm in support. It is about BEING someone who is courageous enough to take a stand, and stay standing. It means having a well-defined sense of right, and the internal strength to defend it. A leader cannot DO this, if he or she cannot BE it. It is an unfortunate truth in business today that we do not find too many people who are so clear about who they are that they are willing to take a firm stand regardless of consequences. But a Legacy Leader® is a ready advocate for what is right, which often involves risk. The word advocator was selected because it carries more strength than defender or supporter. This is about internal commitment to causes, practices and people.

BP4

Defining the Terms

Best Practice 4: Advocator of Differences and Community™		
	Your PERSONAL Definition of These Words	Further understanding of these words:
ADVOCATOR (The "Being")		
DIFFERENCES		
COMMUNITY		

Comments

BP4

An ADVOCATOR stands in support of a cause, a practice or a person on its or their behalf.

DIFFERENCES
DIFFERENCES are those qualities that distinguish people or things from other people or things.

Behaviors and Competencies that distinguish an Advocate of Differences

1. Without reluctance, is able to take a stand of support for people, positions, or causes.
2. Learns how others see the world and individual situations.
3. Actively seeks to develop people to full potential. Is a connoisseur of talent, recognizing the value and contribution each person makes.
4. Seeks opinions of those who may think differently, and values their differences.
5. Seeks common ground/good in an environment of differences.
6. Has teams of individuals with diverse approaches and capabilities.
7. Designs inclusive conversations and recaps for understanding.
8. Advocates for strengths-based culture with everyone in position that matches their strengths.

COMMUNITY
COMMUNITY is a group of people with shared interest in working together to achieve shared success.

Behaviors and Competencies that distinguish an Advocate of Community

1. Sees beyond the boundaries of individuals, teams or departments.
2. Always has success of whole organization in mind.
3. Is knowledgeable about perspectives, strengths and offerings available from all sources.
4. Looks for cross-functional opportunities where unique talent can be developed.
5. Aware of, and believes in, benefits of inclusion.
6. Helps others discover and value their strengths and potential contributions.
7. Has identified his/her own contribution to community.
8. Defends, supports and speaks up for community.

ESSENCE OF BEST PRACTICE 4

1. Creates and maintains ongoing dialogue and involvement with internal/external communities.

2. Promotes inclusion that unites towards common focus.

When your Facilitator assigns you a few of the competencies listed to the left, circle them. Provide notes regarding a "How To" guide to accomplish these points. You may use any of the materials given you to help in this exercise. Draw on your own experiences. Try to provide practical guidelines for how these competencies can be modeled in the workplace. You will be reporting back your "How To's" to the group. You may present your information in any method you choose (teach, do a skit, tell a story, sing a song—it's your choice!)

BP4

The PCSI©

Personal Coaching Styles Inventory (PCSI)©

The PCSI is one method of gathering data to identify differences and strengths of individuals working together in organizations.

From the exercise and presentation what are your key insights about styles?

What are the style definitions?

What is the **Directing Style**?

What is the **Presenting Style**?

What is the **Mediating Style**?

What is the **Strategizing Style**?

NOTES:

BP4

The PCSI©

Personal Coaching Styles Inventory (PCSI)©

The PCSI is one method of gathering data to identify differences and strengths of corporate individuals.

For purposes of this group today, work together to identify the following:

What is the style makeup of this group?

    Who has the predominant **Directing Style?**
    Who has the predominant **Presenting Style?**
    Who has the predominant **Mediating Style?**
    Who has the predominant **Strategizing Style?**

If this were a Project Team, is there enough diversity of style in this group to allow for innovation? Why would that be important?

Summary Questions for this Best Practice:

1. What difference does it make when an employee believes that his/her boss is keenly aware of talents and constantly advocates for their development and use within the organization?

2. What is the best method for identifying strengths, perspectives and styles?

3. What are some ways to begin to determine ways to utilize such abilities?

4. Do you consider yourself an inclusive leader? What examples would you offer for that answer?

5. What impact will such inclusion of diversity make on the organization's bottom line?

NOTE: The PCSI is a styles inventory tool developed by and available through CoachWorks. The Facilitator may choose to use another inventory, and may substitute this page with another worksheet.

BP4

Imperatives to Remember About BP 4

BP 4 Terminal Learning Objectives

As we leave this Best Practice, scan this overview that highlights the learnings taught.

Overview

Definitions

PCSI

BP4

PERSONAL WORK

For Your Own Leadership Position:

For Your Peer Team

1. Do you know the specific talents of your primary peer team?

2. Are you able to easily listen to differing opinions without feeling threatened?

3. Does your peer team have enough diversity of perspective in order to create innovative solutions?

4. Is trust enhanced because of a feeling of community among the members? If not, what would it take to have this happen?

For Your Own Direct Reports:

1. Is the information about your direct reports readily available to you?

2. Have you actively drawn out the strengths of employees for the purpose of having them be completely engaged in their work and utilized fully?

BP4

Case Study Findings

_____
_____
_____
_____
_____
_____
_____
_____
_____
_____
_____
_____
_____
_____
_____
_____
_____
_____
_____
_____
_____
_____
_____
_____
_____
_____
_____
_____

BP4

Case Studies

Differences and Community

Case Study 1: Who's Right For the Team?

Jim Alsop is in trouble. He's heading up a new venture company, a spin-off from a larger company, and seven months into the venture, he can't seem to get the product out the door for timely delivery. Brand new customers are starting to call, very often. It's a small company, just four executives who have worked together for a long time, and a small staff for each. Jim is a take-charge, bottom-line visionary with a background in the product field and he loves new projects. He brought his team from the "mother" company to promote a new product line. Jim thought they had all the right people in place, but is beginning to wonder.

Bill, as the marketing/sales VP, has been doing quite well with the prototype product. He's a charismatic guy, able to easily persuade others because of his personality, but he is also known for his ethics. Greg is the product developer, loves to build new things until he gets them working. He's very direct in style, a Gen X'er that likes to do something new all the time. He's already working on the next line of product with his staff of engineers. He also has the current prototype product in stock to fill the orders. He was originally supposed to get someone on his staff to get the product out, but he's been so busy doing what he likes to do best, that it hasn't worked out that way. Bill has been delivering some of the product, but often complains that he likes to sell, not deliver. Then there's Mary, the financial VP, who is also very persuasive and outgoing, so much so that she sold the venture capitalists on the idea of investing in the spin off. She's responsible for all the financial matters, including paying the 25 new staff members that support the executive team. So far, their financials are okay, but Jim worries it won't be long before the initial capital begins to be depleted.

Jim has called his team to a meeting to discuss the issues. They must make a decision today about what to do to remedy the situation because the consultant from the venture capital company is due early next week for an update meeting. The consultant is aware of the problem and is coming to lend his remedy.

What is the real issue (or issues) they face?

Do they have the right people in place?

What are the different strengths represented?

What will the consultant be saying at the meeting next week?

What would a Legacy Leader do in this case?

BP4

Differences and Community

Case Study 2: The President's Dilemma

DHCI is a global health care company that has been undergoing a turnaround effort over the last year. In order to be more profitable in a highly competitive industry, this 50-year old organization must have an executive team that leads the markets around the world. Roberto, the President, worked his way up through the ranks and has put together a diverse group of executives, about half of whom have been with the company for as long as Roberto has been. Several new faces join him at an offsite meeting this year. One new executive from the Pacific Rim has recently replaced an American who returned to the U.S. At this offsite, Roberto notices that when Fuji speaks, not many of the 15 other team members listen. There are side comments and people reading reports. Roberto listens intently to Fuji and believes that Fuji has very good ideas and insights from which the group could really benefit. Fuji is hampered only by his English language difficulties and Roberto found himself paraphrasing for Fuji so that the group could get such extraordinary input. Roberto knows he needs to intervene in this situation, but how will he do it?

What is the real challenge here?

Why is the rest of the group not listening?

What should Roberto do?

What would a Legacy Leader do to have this be a learning possibility?

BP4

Case Studies

Differences and Community

Case Study 3: Should She Resign?

Chris doesn't fit in very well in her new position as Director of Communications for this regional division of a large defense contractor. Chris is a Gen X'er with lots of energy, boundless ideas and a totally different perspective than most of her peers, who are a good mix of both men and women. Jake, the COO, who was told by the CEO to get some new "blood" in his department to represent them well to the regional community, hired Chris. Chris was hired from a company that has been known for its innovation. She loves to connect with the community and is proud of the new organization for which she works.

However, after 6 long months of offering her best to the group, she has made no headway in having her ideas accepted or even respected. She sits in meetings and hears no one else offering up possibilities or doing anything except reporting on what their own department is doing. When she talks to Jake, he often tells her why they can't do it that way. She believes there is not a place for her here.

So she has scheduled a meeting with Jake next week to ask for his help, or to offer her plans for leaving the company.

What should Chris ask for from Jake?

What are her prospects with this peer group and can she do anything about it herself?

What should Jake do when confronted with this?

What will the CEO say to Jake if he must tell him that Chris is leaving?

What would a Legacy Leader do in this situation, both from Chris's point of view as well as Jake's view?

Where do these events leave a community who depends on this company for jobs and who wants them to succeed?

BP4

Case Studies

Differences and Community

Case Study 4: Trial by Fire for the New President

This company has just had a major reorganization after merger between two pharmaceutical companies. There has been much fallout and all the remaining employees know that a new President is on the way, they just don't know who it will be. The current President has seen them through the merger and now knows he is not the right person to take the company from here.

Then, just last week, a news organization did a major exposé on the ethical procedures for hiring that one of the merged companies practiced pre-merger. The exposé was about several multinational companies, not just this one. It seems that Americans were always placed in charge of the European and Pacific Rim sites, without thought to hiring local leaders who were highly qualified as well as having knowledge of the community culture in their area.

Does this company need to bend to the news report and do something different? If so, why?

If you were the new President coming in to lead the company, what would you do about this situation?

What strengths and attributes should be considered for the leaders of these remote sites?

How would a Legacy Leader approach this situation?

Differences and Community

Case Study 5: George at a Major Turning Point

Imagine that you've been employed with the company for 35+ years and have been working your way up to upper levels of leadership. Suddenly, (or at least it seems sudden) there is a new President saying that what is needed from workers is business savvy, flexibility and innovative thinking. This is exactly what happened to George. At 62, he just wants to curl up in a comfort zone and hope for the best while he waits for retirement.

He wonders if he can make the grade. He wonders if his direct reports will be willing to learn. He is fiercely protective of them and the way they work and wants what is best for them. They have followed his lead for a long time. Now he's beginning to think, however, that deciding to hunker down and be resistant to change is probably not going to work too well for himself, or for his people.

And now, the latest thing that's happened is a request from his boss to provide a comprehensive list of strengths, abilities, learning perspectives, communication styles, potential flexibility and possible community interface of each of his employees. The boss says she wants to make sure that all their strengths are appropriately utilized so they will be more satisfied. George realizes he really doesn't know them that well. This will take some work and may scare them, making them feel like they are just being set up to be let go.

What does George need most right now?

How can he do what is asked of him and ensure the trust he has always had with his employees?

Is there a way for him to be positive about this situation?

What does George's boss need to do for him?

If George's boss were a Legacy Leader®, what would she be doing about this situation?

BP4

Differences and Community

Case Study 6: How Do You Get Beyond the Profession For Which You Were Trained?

Terry has been very highly regarded in his company. In his position of Assoc. General Counsel he has become very highly proficient as a corporate lawyer. He was given an office that was not attached to a particular department. The other two lawyers in his small group had offices offsite in other areas. He rarely sees them, and only works directly with his boss, Cody. Cody wants Terry's office close because of the overlap in the work they are doing. But Terry rarely sees him either, although Cody always praises his work and lets him know that he is highly regarded and valued in the company.

What Cody does not know is that Terry is a people person, does not do well (is not happy) working in isolation. Most of the time he feels very alone, with no one to interact with on a regular basis. What Cody also does not know is that Terry has the strong capability and ambition to be a leader who has a group around him with whom he makes decisions. Terry has also become an industry expert with each of the divisional areas he has handled regulatory matters with. Cody may think that keeping Terry in the position of Counsel is best for the company, and after all, who else could they find that could do as well as he does. However, Terry will ultimately move beyond his "lawyering" and into higher levels of leadership.

In the meantime, Terry will either wither on the vine in his current position, or he will move to another company where all of his strengths are valued and where he can be fully readied for leadership in his field of expertise.

What should Terry communicate to his boss? What should he ask for?

What should Cody be doing to retain strong talent?

If either of them were a Legacy Leader, what would each be doing about this situation?

PERSONAL WORK

For Your Own Leadership Position:

For Your Peer Team

1. Do you know the specific talents of your primary peer team?

2. Are you able to easily listen to differing opinions without feeling threatened?

3. Does your peer team have enough diversity of perspective in order to create innovative solutions?

4. Is trust enhanced because of a feeling of community among the members? If not, what would it take to have this happen?

For Your Own Direct Reports:

1. Is the information about your direct reports readily available to you?

2. Have you actively drawn out the strengths of employees for the purpose of having them be completely engaged in their work and utilized fully?

BP4

LLCI Analysis

Name of Coach:

Name of Legacy Leader®:

General Impressions:
(Indicate your overall thoughts and reaction of this Legacy Leader's Competency Inventory)

BEST PRACTICE # 1—Holder of Vision and Values™

STRENGTHS	AREAS FOR IMPROVEMENT

Questions I need to ask:

Specific Recommendations for Competencies:

LLCI Analysis

BEST PRACTICE # 2—Creator of Collaboration and Innovation™

STRENGTHS	AREAS FOR IMPROVEMENT

Questions I need to ask:

Specific Recommendations for Competencies:

BEST PRACTICE # 3—Influencer of Inspiration and Leadership™

STRENGTHS	AREAS FOR IMPROVEMENT

Questions I need to ask:

Specific Recommendations for Competencies:

LLCl Analysis

BEST PRACTICE # 4—Advocator of Differences and Community™

STRENGTHS	AREAS FOR IMPROVEMENT

Questions I need to ask:

Specific Recommendations for Competencies:

BEST PRACTICE # 5—Calibrator of Responsibility and Accountability™

STRENGTHS	AREAS FOR IMPROVEMENT

Questions I need to ask:

Specific Recommendations for Competencies:

Other insights or suggestions based on our conversation:

LLCI Analysis

Sample LLCI Coaching Questions

1. What are your greatest strengths as a leader? Which of the 5 Best Practices was the one you connected to the most? To what do you attribute that connection?

2. Similarly, for the BP that you scored lowest (or have less depth of understanding), what elements need work? Which of the competencies would give you the most leverage if you focused on improving them?

3. For the statements that you marked "*consistently*," can you give me a specific example where you have demonstrated this competency?

4. For those statements that you marked "*occasionally*" or "*not at all*", can you think of opportunities that you missed where this competency would have been effective? How could you capitalize on this type of opportunity in the future?

5. What is the data telling **you**? What surprises (if any) did you experience as you evaluated your competencies as you were learning about the Best Practices this week? Does your assessment of your competencies in the LLCI correlate to other feedback you've received (360 feedback, leadership surveys, other measures)?

6. When analyzing your data, which are the top 3 areas of focus for you? Let's brainstorm for a few minutes on ways/options for you to practice these competencies.

7. What are the obstacles (personal and organizational) that are holding you back from being a true Legacy Leader?

8. How does your assessment of this data fit with your personal goals? What elements reinforce each other as strong items to add to your Action Plan?

9. If you had more time, money, resources (i.e. no constraints), what would you put into practice and when? What would be the expected outcome? Will you do it?

10. Who else can shed light on this data? How can you use other relationship resources to help you achieve your goals?

Development Plan

Key Inputs:

- ☐ Legacy Leadership Competency Inventory (LLCI)™ results
- ☐ Team Teach Reviews
- ☐ Leader Partner Feedback
- ☐ Insights gained from Networking
- ☐ My Reflections from the Field Guide – my AHA's
- ☐ My past experiences, skills and self-knowledge

SECTION 1: Commitments to Self

Key captures for each Best Practice. Complete the following five mini-tables, one for each of the 5 Best Practices, and the questions following the tables.

1

BEST PRACTICE #1—Holder of Vision and Values™
A HOLDER "keeps in hand" those things that are important, embracing and encouraging their remembrance.
What I already knew about this Best Practice:
What I want to remember about this Best Practice:
Turn to your responses in the LLCI booklet for this Best Practice. In the following spaces, list 1-2 competencies that are STRONG (that I want to continue to model) and then AREAS TO IMPROVE.
STRENGTH:
DEVELOPMENT OPPORTUNITY:

Development Plan

2

BEST PRACTICE #2—Creator of Collaboration and Innovation™
A CREATOR causes something to "come into being" through original or inventive means.

What I already knew about this Best Practice:

What I want to remember about this Best Practice:

Turn to your responses in the LLCI booklet for this Best Practice. In the following spaces, list 1-2 competencies that are STRONG (that I want to continue to model) and then AREAS TO IMPROVE.

STRENGTH:

DEVELOPMENT OPPORTUNITY:

3

BEST PRACTICE #3—Influencer of Inspiration and Leadership™
An INFLUENCER brings about a desired effect in others, by direct or indirect means.

What I already knew about this Best Practice:

What I want to remember about this Best Practice:

Turn to your responses in the LLCI booklet for this Best Practice. In the following spaces, list 1-2 competencies that are STRONG (that I want to continue to model) and then AREAS TO IMPROVE.

STRENGTH:

DEVELOPMENT OPPORTUNITY:

Development Plan

4

BEST PRACTICE #4—Advocator of Differences and Community™
An ADVOCATOR stands in support of a cause, a practice or a person on its or their behalf.

What I already knew about this Best Practice:

What I want to remember about this Best Practice:

Turn to your responses in the LLCI booklet for this Best Practice. In the following spaces, list 1-2 competencies that are STRONG (that I want to continue to model) and then AREAS TO IMPROVE.

STRENGTH:

DEVELOPMENT OPPORTUNITY:

5

BEST PRACTICE #5—Calibrator of Responsibility and Accountability™
A CALIBRATOR "sets the mark" for the quantitative measurement of success.

What I already knew about this Best Practice:

What I want to remember about this Best Practice:

Turn to your responses in the LLCI booklet for this Best Practice. In the following spaces, list 1-2 competencies that are STRONG (that I want to continue to model) and then AREAS TO IMPROVE.

STRENGTH:

DEVELOPMENT OPPORTUNITY:

Development Plan

Question

What are my **strengths** as a Legacy Leader®? What are the elements of Legacy Leadership® that are like "falling off a log" to me? How can I further develop and use these strengths in my current position?

Question

If I were making a "to do" list for my personal leadership development as a Legacy Leader®, what are my **top three** commitments to myself?

1.

2.

3.

NOTES

Development Plan

SECTION 2: Commitment to Grow Other Leaders

If the fundamental premise of a Legacy Leader® is to teach others to be Legacy Leaders®, then:

Question

What opportunities are available to me *right now* to teach LL to others?

Question

What LL supporting materials and techniques will I use to grow other leaders?

Question

How will I integrate Storytelling into my Legacy Leadership® portfolio?

Question

Which leaders in my organization/practice/workplace will I grow as Legacy Leaders® in the next month?

Development Plan

Question

With whom will I share this Action Plan and when?

Question

How will I know when I am a Legacy Leader? What will success look like?

My assessment of myself as a Legacy Leader® at the BEGINNING of the Institute:

0 — 1 — 2 — 3 — 4 — 5 — 6 — 7 — 8 — 9 — 10
0 = "I am familiar with the concepts"　　　　　　　　　　"I behave this way daily" = 10

My assessment of myself as a Legacy Leader® now:

0 — 1 — 2 — 3 — 4 — 5 — 6 — 7 — 8 — 9 — 10
0 = "I am familiar with the concepts"　　　　　　　　　　"I behave this way daily" = 10

Relationships and Resources I can call upon for my development:

Signed:_____ Date:_____

What Legacy Leaders® Need to:
Know, Believe and Do

BEST PRACTICE	Know	Believe	Do
	Essence: Know that their role is to develop others, who develop others	**Essence:** Believe that the major role of the leader is to see that others develop their full potential	**Essence:** Constantly see opportunities to develop people
Best Practice #1 Holder of Vision and Values™	o Know their own vision and values as a human being o Know who they are and purpose for being here. o Know and align with organizational goals	o Believe that without clear direction (from both vision and values) there is no leadership	o Develop and embody the vision/values that clearly establish direction
Best Practice #2 Creator of Collaboration and Innovation™	o Know how to listen and draw out what others don't know is within them. o Know they don't have to have the answers o Know that best group thinking is better than individual thinking o Know how to create an environment of trust	o Believe that better, newer creative/innovative solutions come from tapping the best thinking from everyone	o Create and sustain a trusting environment where it's okay to be brilliant as well as make mistakes.
Best Practice #3 Influencer of Inspiration and Leadership™	o Know that relationships are the fundamental building blocks of leadership o Know that everything they do and say influences others o Know what is inspiring to them personally o Know that in all times (good and bad) it takes courage to lead	o Believe that one must be inspired to inspire others o Believe that relationships are the heart of leadership	o Make sustainable relationships
Best Practice #4 Advocator of Differences and Community™	o Know that each and every person has a significant contribution to make o Know that people need community and to be acknowledged within it o Know that people work better from their strengths o Know that it may not be popular taking a stand for people. o Know that inclusive works better than exclusive	o Believe that everyone has a positive contribution to make o Believe that a Legacy Leader is a respecter of persons o Believe there is a richness in diversity of perspectives	o Discern differences/uniquenesses in perspective and strengths and utilize the differences in positive outcomes o Create synergistic relationships in teams and groups of stakeholders
Best Practice #5 Calibrator of Responsibility and Accountability™	o Know that they must execute against vision o Know that things are constantly changing and constant monitoring of trends and recalibration is necessary o Know that they must be personally responsible and accountable o Know that in order to gain commitment from workers, there must be clarity about expectations	o Believe that if people would keep their word, we could put our world (and our organizations) together better than they have ever been. o Believe that they are personally responsible for their sphere of influence	o Develop and execute against the vision and deliver on expectations through use of quality processes and methods o **Note: The "doing" part here is a 50,000' view. Refer to back of the LL Model.**

House of Legacy

The Relationship of the Five Best Practices

How do you build your House of Legacy? Each of the five shapes below represents one of the 5 Best Practices. Using the concept of building a house, which shape would represent which Best Practice to you? How do you see the interrelationship of the Best Practices in this exercise? Label the shapes below, and provide bullet points for your justification and reasoning. Be prepared to share.

Homework

Section Homework

Choose any or ALL of the following:

- Go back and answer any questions still not discussed at the end of the day for the Best Practice 4 Case Studies, and the personal work page there.

- If time did not allow it during the Institute, review the PCSI content (or other tool used during Institute), answer the questions, and determine your type. Review the other types for interaction, collaboration and innovation ideas applicable to your situation and your teammates.

Use this page to record any thoughts as you do these exercises.

Legacy Leadership® Review

Participant Name: _____ Date: _____

1. **Fill in the blanks to complete the *5 Best Practices:***
   a. Advocator of _____ and Community
   b. _____ of Vision and Values
   c. Influencer of Inspiration and _____
   d. _____ of Collaboration and _____
   e. Calibrator of _____ and Accountability

2. **Which of the following *Readiness Indicators* demonstrate that a *Professional* is a prime candidate for Legacy Leadership®?**
   ____ I would like to inspire others, and be inspired myself, to see and reach the greatest potentials.
   ____ I would like my work to be fun, and also promote that environment for others.
   ____ I would like to grow my skills to advance my career options.
   ____ I am ready to change my attitudes and break out of old habits to create new successes.
   ____ I would like to become more of a mentor, modeling leadership practices and attitudes to others in my team.
   ____ All of the above.

3. **Which of the following are *three Behaviors and Competencies* that distinguish a *Holder of Values:***
   ____ Models authenticity. Personal and professional life is seamless.
   ____ Actively seeks to lift up others, even those "outside" immediate corporate or departmental lines.
   ____ Encourages others to develop, define and live personal values.
   ____ Is self-inspired, and knows what inspires others.
   ____ Respects others.
   ____ "Walks the talk" of personal core values.

4. **A Legacy Leader® who is a *Creator of Collaboration* believes in spontaneous or impromptu brainstorming sessions, which are freeform, open-ended and completely unstructured.**
   _____ True   _____ False

5. **What is the *definition of a LegacyShift*™? Give one example.**

6. **Which of the following is NOT an element of a good *Story:***
   ____ explanation of state of affairs
   ____ an outcome
   ____ both a hero and a heroine
   ____ setting of characters
   ____ none of the above

Legacy Leadership® Review

7. **Which *Best Practice* is categorized with these *Challenges or Potential Barriers:***
   - Leaders that do not fulfill their own responsibilities
   - Lack of compassion and caring for people
   - No roadmap
   - Forgetting the customer
   - ___ BP#1 – Holder of Vision and Values ™
   - ___ BP#2 – Creator of Collaboration and Innovation ™
   - ___ BP#3 – Influencer of Inspiration and Leadership ™
   - ___ BP#4 – Advocator of Differences and Community ™
   - ___ BP#5 – Calibrator of Responsibility and Accountability ™

8. **Please complete the following *definitions:***
   Inspiration
   Inspiration is the process of:

   Leadership
   Leadership is the process of:

   Which Best Practice embodies Inspiration and Leadership? (circle one)   1   2   3   4   5

9. **The following *Language Questions are critical to Best Practice 5 – Calibrator of Responsibility and Accountability:*** _____ True _____ False:
   - Questions that encourage all individual parts of "community" to contribute their very best to the process.
   - Questions that seek to determine if actions measure up to standards and levels of excellence.

10. **Provide one *Legacy Step* for each Best Practice** (one that particularly resonates with you personally):

    BP#1 – _____

    BP#2 – _____

    BP#3 – _____

    BP#4 – _____

    BP#5 – _____

11. **How would you advise another Legacy Leader® to embrace the concept of *Reflection* and journaling?**

12. Which of the following Legacy Leadership® statements are true? *(Check all that apply.)*

___ it's about individuals, the heart of relationships
___ it's about distinction and inclusion
___ it's about direction and commitment
___ it's about doing what's best for people, no matter what
___ it's about the environment of working relations
___ it's about execution and performance
___ none of the above
___ all of the above

13. Match the following *Expected Outcomes* to the associated Best Practice:

___ a. stretches to be the best   1. Holder
___ b. has meaning and purpose for efforts   2. Creator
___ c. puts ego aside to hear brilliance of others   3. Influencer
___ d. loyal customers   4. Advocator
___ e. reputation attractive to employees   5. Calibrator

14. *An Advocator of Differences* ...

___ seeks to discover how others see the world and individual situations **OR**
___ always has the success of the whole organization in mind

15. *An Advocator of Community* ...

___ sees beyond the boundaries of individuals, teams or departments **OR**
___ helps ensure that the right people are in the right positions within the organization

16. Name 3 Resources to demonstrate the business impact of Legacy Leadership® on the bottom line (*Business Applications for Legacy Leadership®*):

17. How can the *LLCI* assist you to grow other leaders? *(Check all that apply)*:

___ tool to determine the business issues of other leaders
___ assessment of a great leader
___ 360 view of a leader's strengths and weaknesses
___ to benchmark their level of competency in each of the 5 Best Practice contexts
___ pass/fail of a leader's key competencies

18. Name one *Essence Statement* for each Best Practice:

BP#1 – _____

BP#2 – _____

BP#3 – _____

BP#4 – _____

BP#5 – _____

19. An *Influencer of Inspiration and Leadership*™ builds positive, meaningful relationships with energy, enables others to lead through positive modeling and recognizes, acknowledges and inspires others.

_____ True   _____ False

20. Which of the following *Indicators* demonstrate that an *Organization* is *ready* for Legacy Leadership®?

____ The Company wants leadership that sets a clear direction.
____ The Company wants a healthier bottom line.
____ The Company wants to attract and retain high potential employees.
____ The Company wants to increase loyalty among customers.
____ The Company is willing to expand out from old boundaries and learn new patterns for success.
____ The Company would like a reputation in the outside corporate world of integrity and employee value.
____ All of the above.

Score: _____

This is the end of the formal Legacy Leadership® Review. If there is time remaining, you may choose to complete the remaining OPTIONAL questions to give you added insight into Legacy Leadership® and the Best Practices.

Optional Development Questions

21. **For each Best Practice, select *one Challenge* that you feel will be <u>easiest</u> for you to overcome to get off to a fast start:**

BP#1 – Holder of Vision and Values

BP#2 – Creator of Collaboration and Innovation

BP#3 - Influencer of Inspiration and Leadership

BP#4 – Advocator of Differences and Community

BP#5 – Calibrator of Responsibility and Accountability

22. **Now select *one Challenge* that you feel may take <u>additional effort</u>, resources, time or a paradigm shift for it to be overcome.**

BP#1 – Holder of Vision and Values

BP#2 – Creator of Collaboration and Innovation

BP#3 - Influencer of Inspiration and Leadership

BP#4 – Advocator of Differences and Community

BP#5 – Calibrator of Responsibility and Accountability

Notes

More...

Personal Work

Make the Case for Legacy Leadership®

Detail here how you would present the case for Legacy Leadership® within your, or any other organization. Use what you have learned in this Institute and your own ideas and experience to outline a presentation for the benefits of Legacy Leadership®. This could be considered your "elevator speech" where you make the case for Legacy Leadership® to someone while riding up 30 stories.

Personal Work

My Personal Thoughts

Answer the following questions, either in complete sentences or bullet points:

1. Why do I believe Legacy Leadership® is a good approach to today's corporate leadership dilemma?

2. Why does Legacy Leadership® appeal to me, and why do I think people should be educated and experienced in it?

3. What are the core elements of the 5 Best Practices that make this plan unique?

Personal Work

My Knowledge of Legacy Leadership®

Summarize your knowledge of Legacy Leadership and the 5 Best Practices by writing brief statements, based on your current understanding and experiences, of the following 5 BPs. Indicate not only your knowledge, but also your "heart" understanding of these Best Practices (your personal thoughts of each).

BP#1 – Holder of Vision and Values

BP#2 – Creator of Collaboration and Innovation

BP#3 - Influencer of Inspiration and Leadership

BP#4 – Advocator of Differences and Community

BP#5 – Calibrator of Responsibility and Accountability

Personal Work

Putting It To Work

Read the chart on the following page. How can you use these questions to incorporate Legacy Leadership® into your particular professional situation? Be specific, name people, teams, scenarios, etc. Add any other questions that you feel are appropriate to the list, and to your situation.

How can you also use these questions to uncover the need for Legacy Leadership® in an organization?

Developing the Art of Asking Leadership Questions

Leaders constantly model leadership competencies. One of the most important skills is the ability and courage to ask the tough and thought-provoking questions that create an environment for innovation within the team. There is an art to doing this. Challenge yourself to develop the art.

These questions can be used both in private conversations as well as team meetings. In the columns below, are suggestions to guide you in developing a repertoire of questions within the various areas of Legacy Leadership® competencies. As you practice, add more as you gain proficiency in this art.

Best Practice #1 Holder of Vision and Values™	Best Practice #2 Creator of Collaboration and Innovation™	Best Practice #3 Influencer of Inspiration and Leadership™	Best Practice #4 Advocator of Differences and Community™	Best Practice #5 Calibrator of Responsibility and Accountability™
▪ How does this forward our strategic vision? ▪ How would that approach get us to our goal competitively? ▪ What needs to happen so that we best serve the customer? ▪ How does this ___ X ___ get us closer to where we want to be? ▪ How does this fit with (match) what is being done in ___ X ___ (another business unit)? ▪ What is our message? ▪ Does this build shareholder value? ▪ What questions will we be asking ourselves about this next year?	▪ How is this unique to anything you've done before? ▪ What will we do to leverage what we've already been doing? ▪ What is being done in other industries? Or not being done that could be? ▪ Let's create something even beyond this. What hasn't been done before? ▪ How can we construct the future so that this has a better outcome next time?	**Leader asks him/ herself:** ▪ How have I acknowledged each and every one? ▪ How have I made each person feel extraordinary? ▪ How have I let them know that I expect extraordinariness? ▪ What strengths do they need to be recognized for? ▪ How are we leveraging our successes? ▪ How are you taking this message back to your people?	▪ What resources can we draw upon to make this even better? ▪ What strengths within this team are best suited for this project? ▪ Who in the ranks needs to help us get this message out? ▪ What do each of you want to contribute to this conversation? ▪ What would it take to get going on this?	▪ What are the pros and cons of this approach? ▪ What would keep us from being successful with this? ▪ What outcomes do we want from this? ▪ What are our successes? (What has worked and what could work better?) ▪ Have we tied down the "what by when by whom?" ▪ Who else needs to be involved with this?

Add additional questions...

Additional Resources

Business Applications for Legacy Leadership®

What thought Leaders have said, and continue to say, about important things to keep 'top of mind' when leading organizations / teams.

(NOTE: We realize that the earlier quotes and references offered here may seem somewhat 'dated' since we first collected them. However, what is contained in them is NOT dated. These are timeless concepts and strategic thoughts for effective and long lasting success, and significance, in organizations. Rather than replace them with newer quotes that will also age in time, we have decided to leave these so that you may benefit from their important content — and have added to them.)

"Leading edge training firms (those that focus on human performance practices, employee training and expenditures, evaluation of offerings) reported better levels of performance on such measures as sales, overall profitability, and the quality of products and services."

ASTD (American Society for Training & Development)
Benchmarking Service, 1998

"We believe companies can increase their market cap 50% in 3 years. Steve Macadam at Georgia-Pacific changed <u>20</u> of his <u>40</u> box plant managers to put more talented, higher paid managers in charge. He increased profitability from $25 million to $80 million in 2 years."

Ed Michaels, War for Talent (05.17.00)

"Courage is not simply one of the virtues but a form of every virtue at the testing point, which means at the point of highest reality."

C.S. Lewis

"Employee motivation and retention are complex issues and superficial solutions just don't work. Companies that take the easy way out will lose in the long run with high turnover costs."

Penton Publishing, 1999

"Hewlett Packard: No Commands"
Dave Packard and Bill Hewlett started their company in 1938, keenly influenced by the Depression and the importance of job security. Hewlett-Packard grew slowly--by 1951 it had just 215 employees--so Dave and Bill (they insisted on first names) got to know everyone personally. Maintaining those values as the company grew helped shape the now famous HP Way, a management style (codified in 1957) focused on sensitivity to employees. HP eschewed offices for cubicles, which allowed managers to manage by "walking around," as Packard demonstrates, above, in the 1970s. The company's benefits plan was the envy of workers everywhere, and in 1973 HP became the first large American company to offer flextime, a policy that Packard called the "essence of respect for and trust in people." Former CEO Lewis Platt once told FORTUNE that "in the HP environment, you really can't order people to do anything." That also meant it was hard to move the whole company in one direction--one reason Platt sought out Carly Fiorina from Lucent to succeed him as CEO. Fiorina has whipped up a whirlwind at HP, but she knows the HP Way is something she can't reinvent. The folks at HP call her Carly, proof that some things never change."

Fortune's 100 Best Companies to Work For, 2001
Profile of HP - #19 on the list

Employees who rated their boss's performance as poor and said they were likely to look for a new job: 40%. Employees who rated their boss's performance as excellent and said they were likely to look for a new job: 11%."

Spherion and Lou Harris Associates, 1999

"What attracts the best employees to a company, and what makes them stay?" These are two of the oldest questions in the business world, and maybe the most important.

The Gallup Organization of Princeton, N.J. claims to have answered them, once and for all. The question-polling company has identified 12 questions that appear to measure the "core elements" needed to attract and keep the most loyal, productive and talented employees.

Gallup culled these dozen from the multitude of questions it has asked in interviews with more than **a million employees during the past 25 years.** Using factor analysis, regression analysis, concurrent validity studies, focus groups and follow-on interviews, Gallup statisticians isolated the questions that most accurately measure the likelihood that a given workplace will attract and keep the best people.

The exact wording of the questions is important:

1. Do I know what is expected of me at work?
2. Do I have the materials and equipment I need to do my work right?
3. At work, do I have the opportunity to do what I do best everyday?
4. In the last seven days, have I received recognition or praise for good work?
5. Does my supervisor, or someone at work, seem to care about me as a person?
6. Is there someone at work who encourages my development?
7. At work, do my opinions seem to count?
8. Does the mission of my company make me feel like my work is important?
9. Are my co-workers committed to doing quality work?
10. Do I have a best friend at work?
11. In the last six months, have I talked with someone about my progress?
12. At work, have I had opportunities to learn and grow?"

First, Break All the Rules,
by Marcus Buckingham, Curt Coffman, 1999

"A company's investment in providing coaching to it's executives realized an average return on investment (ROI) of almost six times the cost of coaching. Among the benefits to executives who received coaching were improved:
- Working relationships with direct reports (reported by 77% of executives)
- Working relationships with immediate supervisors (71%)
- Teamwork (67%)
- Working relationships with peers (63%)
- Job satisfaction (61%)
- Conflict reduction (52%)
- Organizational commitment (44%)
- Working relationships with clients (37%)"

Scientific Research on the Effects of Coaching,
Modis Professional Services, Olivero, Bane, Kopelman on the ManchesterInc. Study, 2001

"Randall MacDonald led the Human Resources team as Executive Vice President—Human Resources and Administration at GTE (now part of Verizon Communications). He wanted to prove what he knew: since talent had become a primary business driver in the competitive telecommunications industry, HR was adding significant value to the organization. "We had leading-edge strategy, but no real evidence of results," according to MacDonald.

Today, all that has changed. Working with Hewitt, GTE developed an award-winning HR Balanced Scorecard and has begun work on a custom online measurement system. By translating HR vision and strategy directly to GTE business objectives through the scorecard, GTE's HR organization has been effective in communicating its strategy, motivating and tracking performance against organization and business goals, and aligning its HR employees with the business strategy.

"Today, HR professionals are in jobs where they can make a difference. They are deployed on strategically important issues, like attracting talent and leadership to the organization. And the HR organization is positioned to provide information on work-force issues to managers in time for them to make the best possible decisions," concludes Bob Gandossy, Global Practice Leader, who worked with GTE on their measurement strategy.

MacDonald, who has since joined IBM in a senior HR role, continues to be an avid proponent of HR measurement. He encourages his colleagues at other companies to jump on the metrics bandwagon. "We have an obligation to show what the bottom-line relationships are between people and business results. My advice is—do it, and do it now."

Hewitt, 2000

"We did research with Andersen Consulting and interviewed over 200 high potential leaders from 120 countries around the world. Some of the things that we found out are: One, it's very important to provide a sense of challenge so people feel excitement and enthusiasm about what they're doing and the mission of their work, the work itself. Two, it's very important to focus on people, the importance of giving them recognition. You need to treat them as team members, and make sure they're involved. Three, it's very important that people have the opportunity to follow their dreams, and that the companies have flexibility in HR systems, so that employees have the opportunity to operate successfully as free agents in a big company."

Excerpted from an Interview with Marshall Goldsmith, 2001

"Studying retention of High Value Employees, using an importance scale of 0-6 and 30 categories (grouped into Work-Life Balance, Organizational Environment, Compensation and Benefits and Work Environment), the single most important attribute in career decisions is **manager quality** (average importance of 5.02)– least likely to be traded away for any other attribute. This was followed by Base Salary (4.58), External Equity (4.22) and Company Reputation (3.64)."

Corporate Leadership Council,
Workforce Commitment Series, 1999

Trend Alert: Leadership Replacing Management
"A significant shift is underway in the business environment. Workers no longer want to be managed. They demand leadership, which requires a whole different set of skills.

Over the past few years, there has been a lot of talk about the differences between leadership and management. And that is the problem. Workers have heard talk, but have not seen action. They are looking for a change in the practices of their superiors, and they are not satisfied with the progress.

To workers, as well as theorists and business school professors, leadership means letting go. Leadership means giving workers more responsibility, more freedom, more power, and more accountability. In the real world, executives, managers, and supervisors are still managing . . . even as they call themselves leaders. Managing includes directing, organizing the work of others, close monitoring, and discipline.

The techniques of management impede corporate growth, especially when desired growth requires original thinking, creativity, innovation, and risk-taking. Such behaviors are very difficult in a traditional management environment. Yet growth is essential in today's competitive, fast-moving world. Growth in products and services, technology, business relationships, market penetration and market share, and the capacity of the company and its workforce are vital just to keep up!

To survive-and thrive-in the fast-changing business environments of today and tomorrow, the practice of leadership can make a substantial difference. Without enough people available to do all the jobs, workers must be empowered to take whatever actions are necessary to accomplish work and serve customers. With fewer people to accomplish the same-or more-work, employers must find new ways of doing things. Leadership.

Problem: Most people in charge of companies, or sections of companies, are more comfortable with management than they are with leadership. They must change. They must learn how to be leaders, while they are almost overwhelmed with the demands of work that must still be done everyday.

Roger and Joyce Herman, 2001

"People join companies and leave managers."

Gallup, 2000

"The ultimate test for a leader is not whether he or she can make smart decisions and take decisive action, but whether he or she can teach others to be leaders and build and organization that remains successful even when he or she is not around. The key ability of winning organizations and winning leaders is creating leaders."

Noel M. Tichy, The Leadership Engine, 1998

"There are two worlds; the world that we can measure with line and rule, and the world we feel with our hearts and imagination."

Leigh Hunt

Andy Pearson Finds Love

"Twenty years ago, as CEO of PepsiCo, Andy Pearson was named one of the 10 toughest bosses in America. Now at Tricon, Pearson has found a new way to lead -- one based on personal humility and employee recognition.

High above Tennessee, the leaders of Tricon Global Restaurants Inc., the largest restaurant chain in the world, are having a casual but strategic conference in one of their corporate jets. Andy Pearson may be sitting in front -- but you'd never know he is one of the two men who run this company. Like all of the others, he wears a golf shirt that bears the logos of their three restaurants: KFC, Pizza Hut, and Taco Bell. He comments lightheartedly on the ideas that the others are advancing about partnering with another food chain -- multibranding in their restaurants for variety. Maybe they'll put a Baskin-Robbins inside Taco Bell. At 30,000 feet, all ideas are good: Pearson isn't about to bring anyone down to earth from up here.

And that in itself is a huge change in Pearson's leadership style. This is the new Andy Pearson, a man who, now in his mid-70s, has transformed himself into a new kind of boss. The old Andy Pearson ran PepsiCo Inc. for nearly 15 years, driving revenues from $1 billion to $8 billion. Back then, he was known for his skills at bringing people down to earth, from any altitude. His chief weapons at the time were fear, surprise, and a fanatical devotion to the numbers. In 1980, Fortune named him one of the 10 toughest bosses in the United States. Pearson was singled out for the relentless demands that he put on his people. As one employee put it, Pearson's talents were often "brutally abrasive."

Twenty years later, Pearson is still proud of having been included in the Fortune article. And he's still unapologetically tough.

These days, Pearson is focused on a different, more positive emotional agenda: "You say to yourself, If I could only unleash the power of everybody in the organization, instead of just a few people, what could we accomplish? We'd be a much better company."

Pearson guides -- but he doesn't control. He used to make a living running companies. Now he governs. The shift is more radical than it may sound.

David Dorsey, Fast Company, August 2001

"In 1982, James E. Burke, the head of Johnson & Johnson, got the most important call of his life. Seven people in Chicago had died when they took Tylenol pills that had been laced with poison. Over the next few days, government officials and Johnson & Johnson executives scrambled to figure out what was happening. For Johnson & Johnson, this was a crucible — the whole world was watching.

Within days it was proved that this was an isolated incident and that J&J was the victim of a terrible crime. In spite of its innocence, J&J continued removing 31 million bottles from store shelves and taking returns from customers. The decision cost the company $100 million."

Noel M. Tichy, The Leadership Engine, 1998

"We are the dreamers and doers; a cast of thousands committed to making magic and making dreams a reality."

DisneyCareers at Disney.com, 2001

"The greatest danger for most of us is not that our aim is too high and we miss it, but that it is too low and we reach it."

Michelangelo

"When I ask CEOs what their greatest concerns are, they typically mention three things: 1) identifying, developing, and retaining top leadership talent; 2) releasing the brain power of people in their workforce; and 3) coping with the uncertainties and complexities of the business environment.

In this article, I want to focus on the first concern because there is no getting away from the colossal significance of effective leadership. Corporations that are perceived as "well led" have increased their stock price over 900 percent compared to 78 percent for firms perceived as poorly led. Although many factors go into being an admired company, the single most important factor is leadership. Leadership is the main instrument for leveraging intellectual capital.

Traits of Emerging Leaders
I keep coming back to five characteristics of exemplary leaders:
1. **They have passion and purpose**
2. **They generate and sustain trust**
3. **They are purveyors of hope and optimism**
4. **They manifest a bias for action**
5. **They keep learning and growing"**

Warren Bennis, founding chairman of The Leadership Institute,
University of Southern California's Marshall School of Business, 1999

Speaking of Loyalty
"While loyalty can mean different things to different people, here are some universal reminders of what loyalty is all about:
- Loyalty that is bought is just as easily sold.
- Loyalty is much easier to talk about than to build.
- Once lost, loyalty is hard to regain.
- Managers who listen find that employees do the same.
- Instead of blind loyalty, look for open-eyed commitment.
- The less loyalty there is, the more supervision will be necessary.
- The better the management, the greater the loyalty.
- Loyalty breeds trust, and vice versa.
- Loyalty is an asset that needs attention; disloyalty gets by on its own.
- Loyalty works both ways: Those who give it expect to receive it."

<u>Source:</u> *Beyond Computing, Friday, May 28, 1999 09:19 AM*

"A key – perhaps *the* key – to leadership is the effective communication of a story."

Howard Gardner, Leading Minds: An Anatomy of Leadership, 1995

Marcus Buckingham Thinks Your Boss Has an Attitude Problem
"Marcus Buckingham teaches CEOs how to get the most out of their people and their organizations. His first lesson: Forget everything you think you know about being a leader.

There is a noble promise at the heart of the new world of business: Everyone has the right to meaningful work, and people who do meaningful work create the most value in the marketplace. Even as the talent wars have fizzled into pink-slip parties, few senior executives would dispute the vital importance of finding, engaging, and developing the best people. Ask any CEO, "What's your company's most precious asset?" Without hesitation, the answer will be, "Our people." Ask the same CEO, "What's the primary source of your competitive advantage?" Chances are, the reply will be, "Our unique culture."

This kind of talk drives Marcus Buckingham nuts. It's not that he disagrees with the sentiments -- he's spent his 15-year career as a pioneering researcher and a global-practice leader at the Gallup Organization, making the link between people, their performance, and business results. What troubles him is the lack of rigor behind the rhetoric. 'There's a juicy irony here," says the 35-year-old Cambridge-educated Brit. "You won't find a CEO who doesn't talk about a 'powerful culture' as a source of competitive advantage. At the same time, you'd be hard-pressed to find a CEO who has much of a clue about the strength of that culture. The corporate world is appallingly bad at capitalizing on the strengths of its people.'

His mission, as he describes it, sounds almost quaint: "to create a better marriage between the dreams of workers and the drive of companies to win." His methodology is anything but quaint. Buckingham has led an effort inside Gallup to crunch three decades' worth of data on worker attitudes into actionable insights on human performance and productivity. First, he and his team tapped into a database of more than 1 million Gallup surveys that focused on workers from around the world. Although these workers had been asked many questions, there was one big question behind the interviews: "What does a strong and vibrant workplace look like?" Buckingham eventually distilled 12 core issues (called the "Q12" in Gallup-speak) that represent a simple barometer of the strength of any work unit.

Next, Buckingham's team ran massive number-crunching studies to analyze how answers to the Q12 shaped hard-core business results. The link between people and performance was vivid. The most "engaged" workplaces (those in the top 25% of Q12 scores) were 50% more likely to have lower turnover, 56% more likely to have higher-than-average customer loyalty, 38% more likely to have above-average productivity, and 27% more likely to report higher profitability.

So what exactly do great managers do? First, the best managers start with a radical assumption: Each person's greatest room for growth is in the area of his greatest strength. It goes back to my last point. Good managers believe that each person is wired in a unique way -- and these managers are fascinated by this individuality. Rather than seek to round it out or fill it in, the best managers do everything they can to sharpen and amplify that uniqueness. And then those managers work with people to help them understand their strengths, to build on them, to give them the confidence to be different.

Satisfaction at work depends on nothing more than self-knowledge. And that gets leaders right back to their main task of engaging their employees at every level. What are you doing to turn your people's talent into the kind of performance that thrills customers, whether those customers are internal or external? The beautiful thing about a culture that is built by focusing on individual strengths is that no one can steal it. And any advantage that's hard to steal is an advantage that lasts.

Excerpted, Polly LaBarr, FastCompany, 2001

One Of Four Workers Would Fire The Boss
"PRINCETON, NJ -- With Labor Day approaching, a new Gallup poll finds that one in four workers -- 24% -- say that if they could do so, they would fire their boss. Overall, the vast majority of Americans -- 86% -- say they are satisfied with their jobs, but among those who are not satisfied, more than half say they would fire their boss. Even among those who are satisfied with their jobs, 20% would still give their boss the ax."

GALLUP NEWS SERVICE, 1997

What Motivates People to Stick Around?
"Companies are seeking to boost profits and to reducing the high cost of employee turnover need to understand what motivates people and prompts them to stick around. If you imagine a whopping salary trumps a boss who knows how to get the most out employees, at least one nationally renowned human resources expert will beg to disagree:

"People's satisfaction with their jobs is determined by a variety of factors, including, most of all, **how they feel about their supervisors,**" says Dr. William Schiemann, President of the Metrus Group, a New Jersey human resources consulting firm. "A company's values play an important part in the equation. People ask themselves *if their company respects them and treats them with dignity.* They ask 'Is there flexibility in how I go about my job? Does the company care about me as an individual?'"

Retaining employees has become so important to a company's competitive advantage that the Conference Board, a New York-based think tank, recently hosted a symposium on the issue for executives and consultants from throughout corporate America.

Recent statistical research confirms that a collaborative corporate culture is key to retaining good people and to increasing sales and profits. The research was performed by Foodmaker Inc. (parent company of Jack in the Box), using a variety of company data, including turnover figures, survey results on quality of work life, employee satisfaction, and same-store sales figures. A positive correlation was found between employees' satisfaction with their supervisors and restaurant sales increases.

"We've always believed that if you treat your people well, they'll take care of your customers, who in turn will take care of your company and enable you to increase profits," says Dr. Mark Blankenship, Foodmaker Vice President of Training. **"This analysis validates that philosophy and really explains why we've been able to achieve two consecutive years of record profits and 17 consecutive quarters of same-store sales increases."**

Business Wire, 1999

"When asked if their workplace most resembled a symphony orchestra, a medieval kingdom or a three-ring circus, **59% of managers and 72% of workers chose either the medieval images or the circus metaphor.**"

Strategies for Preventing Turnover
- InfoWorld Publications, 1999

Employers' New Mantra: Retention

"A growing number of high-performance companies are placing unprecedented value on their employees' job satisfaction. It's not corporate altruism; it's **recognizing the connection between employees and the bottom line. Survey after survey has shown that the attitudes of workers, their supervisors and their employers have a measurable effect on customer satisfaction and revenue.** With labor markets continuing to tighten, employee retention is the single most critical work force management challenge of the future, according to the Corporate Leadership Council.

'Whatever the reasons, workers nowadays feel only a short-term attachment to their employers *and are prone to explore other opportunities, finds a survey by Aon Consulting. Their personal life and career are more important than the firm and its goals.*

Although businesses haven't always acted on the knowledge, psychologists have long been aware of five essentials that people need to be happy in their jobs:

- interesting work
- the need to feel that their work is important
- rewards now
- the promise of greater rewards in the future
- Recognition

Fewer than half the workers surveyed by Aon cite money as the reason for leaving. Most relate to the need for more balance between their work and their personal and family life - part of the larger trend from having it all to finding the right balance.

If working at an upbeat and stimulating company is every employee's dream, then keeping it that way is every manager's challenge."

Trend Letter , January 21, 1999

Co-Authors Carolyn Faqhar and Johngair describe the experience at Sears with this connection between employee satisfaction, customer satisfaction and business results:

"They have identified a strong (.60-.80) correlation between employee satisfaction and customer satisfaction. Their economic model reflects the following formula: If a Sears U.S. store **increases employee satisfaction by .5 units,** in the following quarter customer satisfaction with that store will increase by 2 units and in the next quarter revenue for that store will **increase by 0.5% beyond the Sears national average.**

"Leading companies are recognizing that the success of employees and the success of the organization are closely intertwined. Ensuring employees are seen as drivers of the organization, on equal footing with customers and investors, is central to creating high-performance work environments...making employee satisfaction a central driver in the organization demands that support, resources and systems exist to enable employees to take responsibility for their own success and the success of the organization."

Conference Board of Canada, 1998

Idea in Brief

"The most pernicious half-truth about leadership is that it's just a matter of charisma and vision—you either have it or you don't. The fact of the matter is that leadership skills are not innate. They can be acquired, and honed. But first you have to appreciate how they differ from management skills. Management is about coping with *complexity*; it brings order and predictability to a situation. But that's no longer enough—to succeed, companies must be able to adapt to change. Leadership, then, is about learning how to cope with rapid *change*.

How does this distinction play out?

Management involves planning and budgeting. Leadership involves setting direction.

Management involves organizing and staffing. Leadership involves aligning people.

Management provides control and solves problems. Leadership provides motivation."

Business Review Press, 2011

"Beliefs That Help a Leader Move Up to Level 5"

"If you have managed to move up to Level 4, you are leading at a very high level, higher than 90 percent of all other leaders. But there is still one level higher that may be within your reach. Fewer than 1 percent of all leaders achieve it. To prepare yourself to attempt that final climb and give yourself the best chance of making it to the top, you must first embrace the following beliefs:

1. The Highest Goal of Leadership Is to Develop Leaders, Not Gain Followers or Do Work. When you help other people become leaders, you change their lives. You change the way they see the world. You change their capacity. You increase their potential. You change the way they interact with others. If they become good leaders, you help them improve not only their lives, but also the lives of everyone they touch. I believe that is how you change the world for the better.

2. To Develop Leaders, You Must Create a Leadership Culture. You will not be able to move up to <u>Level 5</u> unless you create a leadership culture. Jim Blanchard did this at Synovus. In an interview with George Barna, Blanchard said, "I think the most important and difficult thing is to create a culture in the organization where leadership is really important. It's important for people in the company to realize that this is a growth-oriented company, and the biggest thing we have to grow here is you, because it's you who will make this company better by your growth. ... So I would think making a culture aware of the significance of developing leaders is valuable."

3. Developing Leaders Is a Life Commitment, Not a Job Commitment. Level 4 leaders develop people. <u>Level 5</u> leaders consistently develop leaders over a lifetime, and the leaders they raise up also develop leaders. It becomes a lifestyle they practice everywhere and at all times, not a program they implement or a task they occasionally practice. Mentoring is a mantle that they wear willingly and they strive to add value to others."

John C. Maxwell, 2012

Across all domains and disciplines, leadership is about the human spirit and human endeavor, underpinned by core values that define character. It is this spirit and endeavor that makes the difference in the form and quality of accomplishment. Howard Gardner has talked about leadership as the capacity to continually create. That capacity, infused with the relentless drive for excellence that is inspirational, creates enduring success- whether we talk about successful sports people, successful artists and composers, successful companies, or successful professionals in any field.

Being Yourself—Every Day

The silent majority of people (the real champions), wake up every morning and bring their best to what they do. They don't necessarily lead companies or countries (in a conventional sense) and they can be found everywhere—from the flower seller to the schoolteacher to the farmer, to moms and dads who believe in character and authenticity and who are driven by a set of values that provide the moral compass for all their actions. We don't write about them often because they occur every day, but if we stop to listen and observe, we can see exemplary behaviors, not in search of recognition but manifesting what is right in the absolute sense and not contextually. It is this vast majority in every organization, in every nation, that can be harnessed to produce extraordinary results, as is empirically evident.

Vini ta Bal i, Spring 2011

"Supporting executives in expanding their intentional leadership development practices and encouraging them to build organizational systems— beyond their individual shared leadership practices—that prioritize talent development are critical to strengthening organizations today and preparing them for leadership transition in the future.

The Daring to Lead survey defined the domains as follows:

Leading self—Have a sense of personal purpose, self-awareness and understanding of personal leadership style, strengths, and abilities.
Leading others inside my organization—Can relate to and understand others, develop them, coordinate their efforts and build commitments.
Leading my organization—Can develop, communicate and manage organizational vision, strategy and priorities. Can problem-solve, make decisions, and manage and communicate change.
External leadership—Can connect to and work with others outside of the organization in order to advance the organization's mission. Includes leading in collaborations, coalitions, partnerships, and other external community relationships."

Daring to Lead 2011: A National Study of Nonprofit Executive Leadership

"People are looking for tangible proof points of **leadership.** And the ability to communicate and inspire people in the face of adversity is a critical part of **leadership.**"

Miles Nadal

Non-profit Execs Face Many Challenges

The recession has amplified the chronic instability of many organizations and thrown non-profit leadership challenges into high relief. Boards and executives are neglecting many critical practices needed to sustain their organizations, according to a new report. Key findings from "Daring to Lead" (www.daringtolead.org):

- Two-thirds of executive directors plan to leave their jobs within five years, yet most boards are under-prepared to select and support new leaders. Only 17% of organizations have a documented succession plan. Only a third (33%) of executives are very confident that their boards will hire the right successor when they leave.

- While 52% of execs are "very happy" with their jobs during their first year, only 37% feel the same way in the following years when job fulfillment and satisfaction with the board drops and they report disillusionment with what boards contribute in terms of support, resources, and strategic thinking.

- Nearly half (46%) of respondents say their organizations have operating reserves of less than three months of expenses. Three months is the minimum level of reserves suggested by experts.

- Coaching is ranked as the most effective professional development strategy, yet only 10% of executives work with a coach.

- 33% of current executives followed a leader who was fired or forced to resign, indicating the frequency of mis-hires and unclear expectations.

- Almost half (45%) of boards haven't reviewed the executive's performance within the past year (one of the board's most essential duties).

Daring to Lead 2011: A National Study of Nonprofit Executive Leadership

"We've identified three areas that are essential to **leadership**, going forward. We call them the "AVCs of **leadership**": authenticity, vision and creativity.

With authenticity, we're saying that authentic **leadership** means having integrity and being transparent. There's an old prevailing attitude in business that if the leader admitted that they didn't know something it was an admission of failure. Well, that's no good anymore. Great leaders must be able to demonstrate an acceptable level of vulnerability, where they're not afraid to say, "I don't know that. And that's why I have the team that I have, because I know I can go to them and ask, 'What do you think?'"
Then, there's vision, which is about giving your workforce a purpose. It's about knowing where you're going. It's something that you're going to put your shoulder behind, something that hits you at an emotional level. And great leaders are able to do that.

Finally, there's creativity. During an economic downturn, organizations have to become more innovative. And to do so, they have to create a climate in which it's safe to fail. You don't want people sitting on their hands in meetings, frightened to say something because they're afraid they'll look silly. You want to be able to create a climate in which you can achieve a common vision."

Steve Eccles - CENTRE FOR CEO LEADERSHIP

Why Do We Become Leaders?

"In my bones, I've always known how important leadership was and is.
The very quality of our lives depends on the quality of leadership—and the quality of the organizations and products they create. We need and seek honest, competent leaders in every area of our lives—government, business, industry, education. We are social animals, and our packs need leaders. Good or bad, they shape our destinies. I sense that leadership is something many people aspire to, whatever role they actually play in life, because authentic leadership elevates whatever organization it is practiced in. *I find that sooner or later in life, all leaders undergo a crucible*—a transformative experience that either prepares them to lead or cultivates in them an *adaptive capacity*—the key attribute for success. In my collaboration with Noel Tichy, I learned that a leader's life is the summation of the leader's judgment calls—making good judgment calls is the primary job of a leader. With good judgment, little else matters. Without good judgment, nothing else matters. And in collaboration with Jim O'Toole and Dan Goleman, I learned that candor is essential for organizational health and that transparency is inevitable in the age of the Internet."

Warren Bennis, 2010

The real power is in making others powerful

Vanity and tyrannical management styles are not uncommon among conductors even today, Zander says, which is perhaps one reason why in at least one survey orchestral players rank only slightly above prison guards in job satisfaction. The truly great conductors, says Zander, are like any other great leader, they understand that their true power "derives from [their] ability to make others powerful." The question to ask, then, is not "How good am I?" but "What makes [this] group lively and engaged?" It is not about gaining sway over your group (or audience or class) so that they will play it the way you envision — or see things your way — but rather the question now becomes how best to enable them to play it beautifully the way they are capable. In presenting — and certainly in teaching — we need to make certain that the audience is engaged so that they may, with our help, find for themselves what is there to be discovered, including the discovery of the possibilities that may be *within them*.

Ben Zander, 2007

"The new leader's job is to create a powerful vision that allows room for things to occur that are as yet undreamed of. The leader must hold the definition of the vision so clearly that all the players involved are able to align with it daily."

Rosamund Stone Zander

"According to Gallup research, which included a meta-analysis of 44 organizations and 10,609 business units, Gallup Polls of the U.S. working population, exit interviews conducted on behalf of several companies, and Gallup's selection research database, most people quit for a few explainable reasons. What's more, a set of engagement elements explains 96% of the attitudes that drive voluntary turnover rates for work units. But the reasons people leave might not be what most bosses think.

According to James K. Harter, Ph.D., Gallup's chief scientist for workplace management, people leave companies because of factors that filter through the local work environment. At least 75% of the reasons for voluntary turnover can be influenced by managers.

(continued next page...)

Continued

The most common answer respondents gave for why they were moving on was for career advance-ment or promotional opportunities (31.5%), while 20.2% said they lacked job fit. And 16.5% said they were leaving, like Anna did, because of management or the general work environment. Much smaller percentages quit because of flexibility or scheduling (7.7%) or job security (1.7%). (See graphic "Why People Change Jobs.")

Notice a pattern? Most of the reasons employees cited for their turnover are things that managers can influence. And managers who can't or won't alter the factors that drive turnover can expect to be writing help-wanted ads in the near future. But there are additional ways to predict turnover in a business unit.

The Top Five Predictors of Turnover

Work units with high potential for turnover send out warning signals, according to Gallup research, but managers and executives must know where to look:

1. The immediate manager. If employees report that their manager's expectations are unclear; or that their manager provides inadequate equipment, materials, or resources; or that opportunities for progress and development are few and far between, watch out: Trouble is on the way.

2. Poor fit to the job. Another sign of trouble appears when employees perceive that they don't have opportunities to do what they do best every day.

3. Coworkers not committed to quality. Watch for employees who perceive that their coworkers are not committed to a high standard of work.

4. Pay and benefits. Engaged employees are far more likely to perceive that they are paid appropriately for the work they do (43%), compared to employees who are disengaged (15%) or actively disengaged (13%). And pay and benefits become a big issue if employees feel that their coworkers aren't committed to quality; they may feel entitled to extra compensation to make up the difference or to make them feel like they are truly valued by their employer.

5. Connection to the organization or to senior management. Another key sign that turnover may be looming appears when employees don't feel a connection to the organization's mission or purpose or its leadership."

Jennifer Robison, Gallup Business Journal

Business Applications for Legacy Leadership®

Top 10 Leadership Quotes

1. *"A leader is one who knows the way, goes the way, and shows the way."* – John C. Maxwell

2. *"A real leader faces the music, even when he doesn't like the tune."* – Anonymous

3. *"All Leadership is influence."* — John C. Maxwell

4. *"Do not go where the path may lead, go instead where there is no path and leave a trail."* — Ralph Waldo Emerson

5. *"Lead me, follow me, or get out of my way."* — General George Patton

6. *"Leadership is the capacity to translate vision into reality."* — Warren Bennis

7. *"Managers help people see themselves as they are; Leaders help people to see themselves better than they are."* — Jim Rohn

8. *"The art of leadership is saying no, not yes. It is very easy to say yes."* — Tony Blair

9. *"The price of greatness is responsibility."* — Winston Churchill

10. *"When the effective leader is finished with his work, the people say it happened naturally."* — Lao Tzu

Sources of Insight: December 2011

Leadership can be defined as one's ability to get others to willingly follow. Every organization needs leaders at every level. Leaders can be found and nurtured if you look for the following character traits.

A leader with **vision** has a clear, vivid picture of where to go, as well as a firm grasp on what success looks like and how to achieve it. But it's not enough to have a vision; leaders must also share it and act upon it. Jack Welch, former chairman and CEO of General Electric Co., said, "Good business leaders create a vision, articulate the vision, passionately own the vision and relentlessly drive it to completion."

A leader must be able to communicate his or her vision in terms that cause followers to buy into it. He or she must communicate clearly and passionately, as passion is contagious.

A good leader must have the discipline to work toward his or her vision single-mindedly, as well as to direct his or her actions and those of the team toward the goal. Action is the mark of a leader. A leader does not suffer "analysis paralysis" but is always doing something in pursuit of the vision, inspiring others to do the same.

David Hakala, 2009

"The key to successful leadership today is influence, not authority." *--Ken Blanchard*

"Leaders are made, they are not born. They are made by hard effort, which is the price which all of us must pay to achieve any goal that is worthwhile." *--Vince Lombardi*

"Good leaders make people feel that they're at the very heart of things, not at the periphery. Everyone feels that he or she makes a difference to the success of the organization. When that happens people feel centered and that gives their work meaning." *--Warren G. Bennis*

"The quality of leadership, more than any other single factor, determines the success or failure of an organization." *--Fred Fiedler and Martin Chemers in Improving Leadership Effectiveness*

"The most dangerous leadership myth is that leaders are born -- that there is a genetic factor to leadership. This myth asserts that people simply either have certain charismatic qualities or not. That's nonsense; in fact, the opposite is true. Leaders are made rather than born." *--Warren G. Bennis*

PROVIDE A POSITIVE WORKING ENVIRONMENT

"Jim Goodnight is the co-founder and President of SAS in Raleigh-Durham, NC. SAS is the largest software development company in the United States. Their progressive work environment and host of family-friendly benefits keeps their turnover rate far below the national average. Jim said, "My assets leave work for home at 5:00 or later each night. It is my job to bring them back each day." Wise executives realize the responsibility for creating a positive work environment cannot be delegated. It starts at the top.

Have you ever worked for a bad boss? One of the main reasons employees quit is the relationship with their first-line supervisor. The fact is many supervisors and managers are unaware how their actions and decisions affect employee turnover. A critical aspect of an effective retention strategy is manager training. Properly trained managers play a major role in an effective recruitment and retention strategy. Managers need the skills, tools, and knowledge to help them understand their employees' retention needs and be able to implement a retention plan designed to increase employee engagement in the organization."

INVOLVE AND ENGAGE

"People may show up for work, but are they engaged and productive? People are more committed and engaged when they can contribute their ideas and suggestions. This gives them a sense of ownership.

The Sony Corporation is known for its ability to create and manufacture new and innovative products. In order to foster the exchange of ideas within departments, they sponsor an annual Idea Exposition. During the exposition, scientists and engineers display projects and ideas they are working on. Open only to Sony's employees, this process creates a healthy climate of innovation and engages all those who participate.

TD Industries in Dallas, TX has a unique way of making its employees feel valued and involved. One wall within the company contains the photographs of all employees who have worked there more than five years. Their "equality" program goes beyond the typical slogans, posters, and HR policies. There are no reserved parking spaces or other perks just for executives -- everyone is an equal. This is one reason why TD Industries was listed by Fortune magazine as one of the "Top 100 Best Places to Work."

Greg Smith

The 7 Principles for Inspiring Employees

If someone asked you for a good synonym for inspiration, what would you say? Some might answer that stimulation is a good substitute. Others might choose influence or encouragement. But by and large, when people think of inspiration, the word that immediately comes to mind is motivation.

But are motivation and inspiration really the same? And from a leadership standpoint, which is better? As leaders, we all want certain things from those who report to us. So do we motivate them to action, or do we inspire them?

Employers are great at motivation, aren't they? Well, depends on who you ask. Sometimes their methods are less than inspiring: they motivate, all right, but through manipulation or threats. "If you don't meet this goal . . ." Even if an organisation does achieve some results this way, they will be short-lived again, because people haven't been inspired.

So, what kinds of actions make the difference between inspiring someone and motivating him or her? And what will that mean to you, as a team leader, department head, or CEO?

(continued next page...)

Leaders who genuinely inspire others do so by tapping into people's dreams then extracting the best from them. This is what is called the "inspiration factor." And whether these leaders just have a knack for inspiring those around them, or they have developed the skill through training or trial and error, the inspiration factor produces more positive transformations than any other leadership trait.

Here are seven principles for inspiring your employees that you can take action on today. Implement one of these principles and make a difference. Implement all seven and change the culture you live and work in.

1. Authenticity - get out of the image management business for yourself and your company. Share with the people in your organisation where you are weak. Verbally express just how much you need them. Let them know that you know your limitations. Invite them to partner with you to get through these difficult times.

2. Connect with Other's Dreams - use these difficult times to uncover the latent dreams and ambitions of your key talent. Tell them you are more committed than ever to helping them get to where they want to go. Be creative in aligning their tasks for today with their dreams for tomorrow.

3. See in Others the Abilities They Don't See in Themselves - take time to be observant. Quit the craziness long enough to notice the talent in those around you. This even works if you are trying to manage up. This principle works best by breaking it down into three steps, notice, name, and nurture. After you have noticed a talent or strength in a person, let them know you noticed it and be specific about what you noticed. Don't just say "I noticed you are a hard worker." Rather, "I notice you care very deeply about making sure the details are in order or I notice you are very articulate on that subject." Look for ways to bring that talent out by providing opportunities and training to support that particular talent.

4. Speak and live with credibility - I also refer to this principle as leading with moral authority. It does not mean much for you to say "let's keep looking for the opportunity ahead" while living in fear and operating with a scarcity mentality.

5. Inspire With Great Stories - this is the principle of overhearing. This is not to be confused with the art of storytelling. The emphasis here is looking and telling stories that have a lesson. What can you learn from the story of a mountain climber? What can you glean from the story of one who has gone from rags to riches or better yet, from riches to rags? Pull your team together today and use story to inspire.

6. Help People to Live on Purpose - remind them that what happens at work is only a portion of their life. As important as that portion is, it is not all that there is to life. Help people write down a vision statement for their life first and then for their job. If work can be a conduit towards that vision for life, great!

7. Create a Culture of Inspiration - following the example of John Wooden, UCLA's iconic coach, become teachers committed to excellence and character development. Chasing numbers and making decisions by looking only at the "bottom line" causes us to be reactive and impulsive.

Focusing on raising the inspiration factor through developing people yields incredible value for stakeholders, customers, and employees alike. Raising the inspiration factor one principle at a time will change the culture of your organisation. A company with a high inspiration factor attracts and keeps good talent and its employees forge long -term profitable relationships with customers.

Terry Barber, 2012

"People (and Organizations) Who Need People"

"During a time of increased global competition, rising uncertainty, and unpredictability, when companies and countries are seeking to rebound, rebuild, and reinvent themselves in the pursuit of growth, CEOs around the world see **Innovation** –of products, processes, organizational designs, and business models – as their most critical challenge. According to the 776 top executives from around the world who responded to The Conference Board CEO Challenge® 2012 survey, **Human Capital-**including acquisition, leadership, employee development, training, and engagement-is the second most "important" challenge that organizations face. The top three strategies selected to meet the Human Capital challenge (grow talent internally; improve leadership development programs; and provide employee training and development) involve internal actions to develop and retain talent already within the company. These strategies reflect the decision to direct increasing resources toward enhancing employee capability to address both short-and long-term needs."

The Conference Board CEO Challenge 2012 – Canada Edition

"The research we conducted for our book, *Building the High-Trust Organization: Strategies for Supporting Five Key Dimensions of Trust,* supported a model of organizational trust with five key drivers:
•• Competence
•• Openness and honesty
•• Concern for employees and stakeholders
•• Reliability
•• Identification
Our research team learned that these five drivers were strong and stable predictors of organizational trust across cultures, languages, industries, and types of organizations.
We believe the five drivers of trust provide concrete guidance for leaders who wish to focus on trust in complex and changing environments. Trust is fundamental to stimulate the innovation, creativity, and risk taking needed to bring about productive change.

The choice to build trust is practical and will bring measurable and positive success. The choice to build trust also speaks to the best in all of us, our high ideals, and our dreams for the future."

Shockley-Zalabak, P. S., & Morreale, S. P.

"There is one thing that is common to every individual, relationship, team, family, organization, nation, economy and civilization throughout the world — one thing which, if removed, will destroy the most powerful government, the most successful business, the most thriving economy, the most influential leadership, the greatest friendship, the strongest character, the deepest love.
On the other hand, if developed and leveraged, that one thing has the potential to create unparalleled success and prosperity in every dimension of life.
That one thing is trust."

R. Covey, Stephen M.

Developing Vision

Write Your Personal Vision Statement

Vision means you have an inner calling, something within that needs to be intentionally identified and stated. It defines how we combine our strengths, our needs and our intentions with enjoyable and fulfilling pursuits. A very brief example of a personal vision statement is "To serve as a catalyst revolutionizing the lives of individuals and their companies." Generally, a personal vision statement will actually include several statements that, taken together, become a singular statement about that person's goals, aims, ambitions, capabilities, beliefs, and desires. To be representative of the person, however, it must be written with all their strengths, needs and intentions in mind.

Developing this personal vision statement requires thoughtful reflection. Consider the following as you develop your statement:

- **The big picture of your life**
- **The things you find most enjoyable**
- **Your strengths**
- **Your needs**
- **Your intentions for life**
- **Your life goals**
- **Your career goals**
- **Where you find significance, fulfillment, passion**
- **Your internal wants and desires (other than material things)**
- **Your wants for others**
- **Your values and beliefs**

After giving careful thought to the above considerations, develop a series of statements using this pattern:

- **ACTION**
  (use a verb to denote what you will DO)

- **OBJECTIVE**
  (the value or aim of the action)

- **WITH WHAT OR WHOM**
  (the thing, person, group of importance to you)

(see next page for exercise)

SAMPLE—
My vision is:

To create
  ACTION (use a verb to denote what you will DO)

positive environments
  OBJECTIVE (the value or aim of the action)

for shifts in individuals or organizations I coach.
  WITH WHAT OR WHOM (the thing, person, group of importance to you)

Vision Statement:
My vision is to create positive environments for shifts in individuals or organizations I coach.

Developing Vision

My Personal Vision Statement

If necessary, write as many statements as you need to identify your vision.

Write these statements here: **My vision is....**

1.

2.

3.

4.

5.

6.

7.

8.

9.

10.

Now here's a real challenge. Can you write a single statement that encompasses all of the above into one comprehensive personal vision statement? Think about it carefully. If you could express your entire vision in one sentence, how would you write it?

Do it here....

Developing Values

The following is excerpted from a more intensive exercise from "Developing Vision and Values" by CoachWorks International. Spend some time looking at these PERSONAL-PROFESSIONAL-SPIRITUAL values and determine which are of highest value to you. Rank them from 1 (lowest value) to 5 (highest value). Continued on next page.

#	VALUE	1	2	3	4	5	COMMENT
WHAT IS OF PERSONAL VALUE TO YOU?							
1	Knowledge of self						
2	Being "together"						
3	Congruent life in all areas						
4	Continued life education						
5	Balanced life						
6	Excellent physical health						
7	Being in control						
8	Personal development						
9	Financial wealth						
10	Positive attitude						
11	Stroked ego						
12	High self-esteem						
13	Personal grooming						
14	Serving others						
15	High energy						
16	Well educated						
17	Personal integrity						
18	Open minded/accepting						
19	Pleasant surroundings						
20	Good relationships						
21							
22							
WHAT IS OF PROFESSIONAL VALUE TO YOU?							
1	Making it to the "top"						
2	Great network						
3	Serving others						
4	Making lots of money						
5	Integrity						
6	Good working relationships						
7	Doing my best						
8	Always learning, developing						
9	Pleasant environment						
10	Being happy at work						
11	Being a leader						
12	Organization						
13	Being focused						
14	Being in control						
15	Fitting in						
16	Adaptive and flexible						
17	Being right						
18	Collaboration						
19	Ethics						
20	Acknowledgement/reward						
21							
22							

Developing Values

#	VALUE	1	2	3	4	5	COMMENT
WHAT IS OF SPIRITUAL VALUE TO YOU?							
1	Having a faith						
2	Knowing about my faith						
3	Living my faith						
4	Continued faith learning						
5	Sharing my faith						
6	Submission to my faith						
7	Being with others of my faith						
8	Understanding my faith						
9	My spiritual future						
10	Spiritual failure of others						
11	Respect for faith of others						
12	Spiritual relationships						
13	Faith-shaped values						
14	Faith values obvious in all areas of my life						
15	Faith integrity (actions match beliefs)						
16	Positive spiritual attitude						
17	Rewarding spiritual life						
18	Faith as foundation for all other activities						
19	Faith as basis for priorities						
20	Contentment with my faith						
21							
22							

Think About This...

1. Where are your "5" responses? What items listed here did you find most valuable to you? Can you comment on why this is so?

2. Did any of your responses surprise you (including your personalized fill-in blanks)? Why?

3. Do you notice any "clustering" of values? That is, certain related items all scoring high or low marks? If so, what and why? (for example, you scored 5s on items all related to sharing, or all related to contentment, or all related to self-esteem, etc.)

Personal Notes

Developing Values
Corporate Values

As a personal or organizational exercise, begin to list (and then add as you think of more) values which you know to be those of your organization, or those you would want to be held by an organization for which you worked. Depending on your situation, you may wish to share this list with others on your team and within your organization as a tool to gain clarity and understanding around your organization's values. If you are not working within an organization at this time, you might choose to use this list as a reference guide for any organization you might serve in the future, or to help clients or others develop their own corporate values.

RANK	CORPORATE VALUE	RANK	CORPORATE VALUE

"Adversity introduces a man to himself."
—unknown

"Nobody's a natural. You work to get good and then work to get better. It's hard to stay on top."

-Paul Coffey, NHL star

"It's surprising how many persons go through life without ever recognizing that their feelings toward other people are largely determined by their feelings toward themselves. If you're not comfortable within yourself, you can't be comfortable with others."
- Sydney J. Harris

"Never doubt that a small group of thoughtful, concerned citizens can change the world. Indeed it is the only thing that ever has."
- Margaret Mead

"Contrary to the cliché, genuinely nice guys most often finish first--or very near it"
-Malcolm Forbes

"A good leader inspires others with confidence in him; a great leader inspires them with confidence in themselves."
-unknown

"I can't imagine a person becoming a success who doesn't give this game of life everything he's got."
-Walter Cronkite

"You can have everything in life you want if you'll just help enough other people to get what they want!"
-Zig Ziglar

"I'm a great believer in luck, and I find the harder I work, the more luck I have."
-Thomas Jefferson

"There is no need to boast of your accomplishments and what you can do. A great man is known, he needs no introduction."
 -unknown

"What you do speaks so loudly that I cannot hear what you say."
-Ralph Waldo Emerson

"The greatest good we can do for others is not to share our riches with them, but to reveal their own.
—unknown

Words of Influence and Inspiration

"You may have a success in life, but then just think of it – what kind of life was it? What good was it – you've never done the thing you wanted to in all your life. I always tell my students, go where your body and soul want to go. When you have the feeling, then stay with it, and don't let anyone throw you off. ... I say, follow your bliss, and don't be afraid, and doors will open where you didn't know they were going to be. ... Wherever you are – if you are following your bliss, you are enjoying that refreshment, that life within you, all the time."
—Joseph Campbell

"Never tell people how to do things. Tell them what to do, and they will surprise you with their ingenuity."
—George S. Patton

"He that gives good advice, builds with one hand; he that gives good counsel and example, builds with both; but he that gives good admonition and bad example, builds with one hand and pulls down with the other."
—Francis Bacon

"Advice is like snow; the softer it falls the longer it dwells upon, and the deeper it sinks into the mind."
—Samuel Taylor Coleridge

"I'd rather fail at doing something I love than succeed at doing something I hate."
—unknown

"It's not hard to make decisions when you know what your values are."
—Roy Disney

"Be willing to make decisions. That's the most important quality in a good leader. Don't fall victim to what I call the Ready-Aim-Aim-Aim Syndrome. You must be willing to fire."
—T. Boone Pickens

"Trust your hunches. They're usually based on facts filed away just below the conscious level."
—Dr. Joyce Brothers

"You must do the thing you think you cannot do."
—Eleanor Roosevelt

"Life is a verb."
—Charlotte Perkins Gilman

"The life which is unexamined is not worth living."
—Plato

"Living is a form of not being sure, not knowing what next or how. The moment you know how, you begin to die a little. The artist never entirely knows. We guess. We may be wrong, but we take leap after leap in the dark."
—Agnes De Mille

"Live your questions now and perhaps, even without knowing it, you will live along some distant day into your answers."
—R. M. Rilke

"The real voyage of discovery consists not in seeking new landscapes, but in having new eyes."
—Marcel Proust

Section Reflection

Section 1

Notes:

Actions I will be taking:

Insights:

With whom will I share this?

More thoughts...

Page 124

Section Reflection

Section 2

Notes:

Actions I will be taking:

Insights:

With whom will I share this?

More thoughts...

Section Reflection

Section 3

Notes:

Actions I will be taking:

Insights:

With whom will I share this?

More thoughts...

Notes

Legacy Leadership® Institute Feedback

Participant Name:_____**Date:**_____

Organization:_____

Institute Attended (Location and Dates)_____

Facilitator(s)_____

---

1 **Overall,** how satisfied are you with the Legacy Leadership® Institute? *(Please circle one:)*

5 = Very Satisfied   4 = Satisfied   3 = Neither Satisfied nor Dissatisfied   2 = Dissatisfied   1 = Very Dissatisfied

---

2 Using the same scale (above), how satisfied are you that the Legacy Leadership Institute met the **STATED OBJECTIVES:** *(Please check appropriate box.)*

Upon completion of this Institute, YOU will be able to:	VD	D	N	S	VS
1. Describe for others the Business Case for integrating Legacy Leadership® into the fabric of all interactions and offerings.					
2. Identify and practice teaching the key competencies and behaviors associated with each of the 5 Best Practices.					
3. Demonstrate the use of the LL Competency Inventory™ (LLCI) as a tool to aid others in developing competencies in other leaders.					
4. Explain your concrete action plan to inspire, equip, gain commitment for and grow Legacy Leaders in all walks of life.					
5. List the linkages between LL principles and positive business results to create the business imperative for pervasive LL in the marketplace.					

---

3 What topics were **MOST valuable** to you (and why?)

_____

_____

_____

_____

---

4 What topics were **LEAST valuable** to you (and why?)

_____

_____

_____

_____

---

5 This program has been designed to meet the needs of Executives, Managers, Coaches and all Leaders. Please help us improve the Institute by providing us with **specific feedback** (circle in the table at right) using the following scale:
1 = Very ineffective
2 = Somewhat ineffective
3 = Neutral
4 = Somewhat effective
5 = Very effective

SPECIFIC AREA FEEDBACK	Circle One				
Content structure and flow	1	2	3	4	5
Environment and materials	1	2	3	4	5
Field Guide	1	2	3	4	5
Use of LLCI	1	2	3	4	5
Quality/Quantity of practical exercises	1	2	3	4	5
Relevance to the business world	1	2	3	4	5
Quality of Facilitation	1	2	3	4	5

6 Based on your experience and satisfaction with the Legacy Leadership Institute, **how likely are you to recommend** this program to other leaders or coaches? *(Please circle one.)*

1 = Very Unlikely   2 = Unlikely   3 = Neutral   4 = Likely   5 = Very Likely

7 Additional Comments

_____
_____
_____
_____
_____
_____
_____
_____
_____
_____
_____
_____
_____
_____
_____
_____
_____
_____

Thank You for your feedback!

ADDITIONAL EXERCISE: AEROTECH BRIEFING

The Aereotech Briefing is included here as an additional resource for those who wish to use it. It is not a mandatory exercise, but the Facilitator's Guide does make reference to it. Its use may depend on your time constraints and your personal selection of exercises most relevant to your group of participants. It was originally designed for use in illustrating the power of Best Practice 2, Creator of Collaboration and Innovation, but can be inserted wherever Facilitators believe it can be most useful.

Aerotech Briefing

COMPANY PROFILE

Aerotech International is a large, multinational ($120 Billion) corporation with headquarters in Houston, Texas. Employing 60,000 employees in 12 sites in the U.S. and Canada with satellite offices in Norway, Italy and Hong Kong, Aerotech has been in business since 1962 and has two main business areas:

1. Large aircraft and part production (i.e.: Boeing 727, 737, 747, Douglas DC-8, DC-9, DC-10, etc.)
2. Aerospace manufacturing (Guided Missiles, Space Vehicles and Parts)

Holding major contracts with large airlines as well as prominent government agencies, Aerotech has been extremely profitable over the years and is proud of its product leadership within the industry and involvement with high profile space projects. However, this lead has been slowly eroding over the last five years, as competition has become incredibly fierce and Aerotech has been slow to invest in e-commerce. In fact, both revenue and profit were reported at their lowest levels ever for the last three quarters in a row.

THE SITUATION

The CEO of Aerotech (Larry Banning) just retired after 32 years of service with the company. He began in Engineering and worked his way up the management ranks to the CEO position, which he has held for the last 8 years. Known as an authoritarian but fair leader, Larry worked closely with his team of 14 direct reports to maintain a strong chain of command. As a retired Air Force Captain, Larry shares a strong military background with most of the senior executive team. In his farewell speech, he thanked them especially as well as key government officials with whom he maintained close personal relationships. He was most proud of the recent expansion into Europe and the future of Aerotech as a truly global company.

Replacing Larry is Chris Day, an external executive hired from a company in a related field appointed by the Board. Chris is 48 years old and has a reputation for "shaking things up" in various corporations in the last few years. This was a bit of a surprise appointment, as the general consensus was that the VP of the Aircraft Division, Casey Chambers, was the natural successor (and Larry's choice). In the first thirty days on the job, Chris has been tireless in learning about Aerotech, visiting every U.S. and Canadian site with plans to visit the overseas operations in the next 3 months. Several town hall meetings to hear ideas from employees at all levels have also been held and Chris has quickly become known as an "idea machine" – sending emails and driving suggestions in all functional areas. Chris also has a reputation as a good communicator, action-oriented and with a high energy level. *You received this memo in your e-mail inbox last week:*

To: Senior Leadership Team

Thanks to all of you who have made my transition into Aerotech smooth and seamless. I've been met with warm welcomes everywhere and I look forward to meeting the whole team before the end of this quarter.

In my travels so far, I've seen well-justified pride from each division and product leadership that is second to none. I've observed a rich history of accomplishments and achievements that has sustained this company through decades of industry ups and downs. I've been impressed by you all.

However, there are some alarming areas of note that require immediate attention. First and foremost, we must turn around the business results NOW. 3 bad quarters in a row is just unacceptable and I'm

BP2

counting on each of you to do whatever it takes to bring Aerotech back to its leadership position. Use the War Rooms that have been set up, and let me know how I can help eliminate barriers for your teams.

What is more concerning to me is the overall lack of collaboration and innovation that I've found. Our two major divisions almost operate as independent companies, missing out on opportunities to collaborate together to save money and share ideas. We say we are an international company, but we are clearly American-led and I believe the European offices go largely unheard in the boardroom. We are missing a huge opportunity in the e-commerce area, and are sticking with "tried and true" while our competitors are jetting ahead of us with innovative new products and services.

From a leadership position, I see a company largely made up of men...how can we attract and retain a more diverse workforce...especially in management? Out of 60,000 employees worldwide, women only make up an unsatisfactory 15%. And our attrition rate overall is 11%, higher than the industry average of 9%. Why are people leaving Aerotech?

I've also attached the Aerospace Industries Association's (AIA) recently published list of the Top 10 Issues in our industry. What are Aerotech's strategies for each of these issues? Who is championing these causes for us?

I don't have the answers to these questions but I know that YOU and your teams do. I've scheduled a board meeting for 10:00 Monday morning and I'm expecting each team to present your creative, outside-of-the-box thinking solutions on how to improve COLLABORATION and INNOVATION to solve these business problems. Please confer with your team and be prepared to present your ideas in a 10 minute summary....Chris

Top Ten Issues

- Support the Presidential Commission on the Future of the U.S. Aerospace Industry

- Support Global Implementation of Commercial Aviation Safety Team Recommendations

- Establish Consensus to Reduce Airplane Noise and Emissions Through ICAO (International Civil Aviation Organization)

- Continue Reform of Export Laws, Regulations and Their Administration

- Adequately Fund Aerospace Procurement and R&D

- Continue Reform of Government/Industry Business Practices

- Facilitate an Integrated E-Business Environment Among Suppliers Customers, and Business Partners

- Develop a Multilateral Plan to Reduce Offsets

- Develop a National Plan to Support the Commercial Space Industry

- Reduce US/EU Aerospace Trade Tensions

BP2

Aerotech Organization Chart

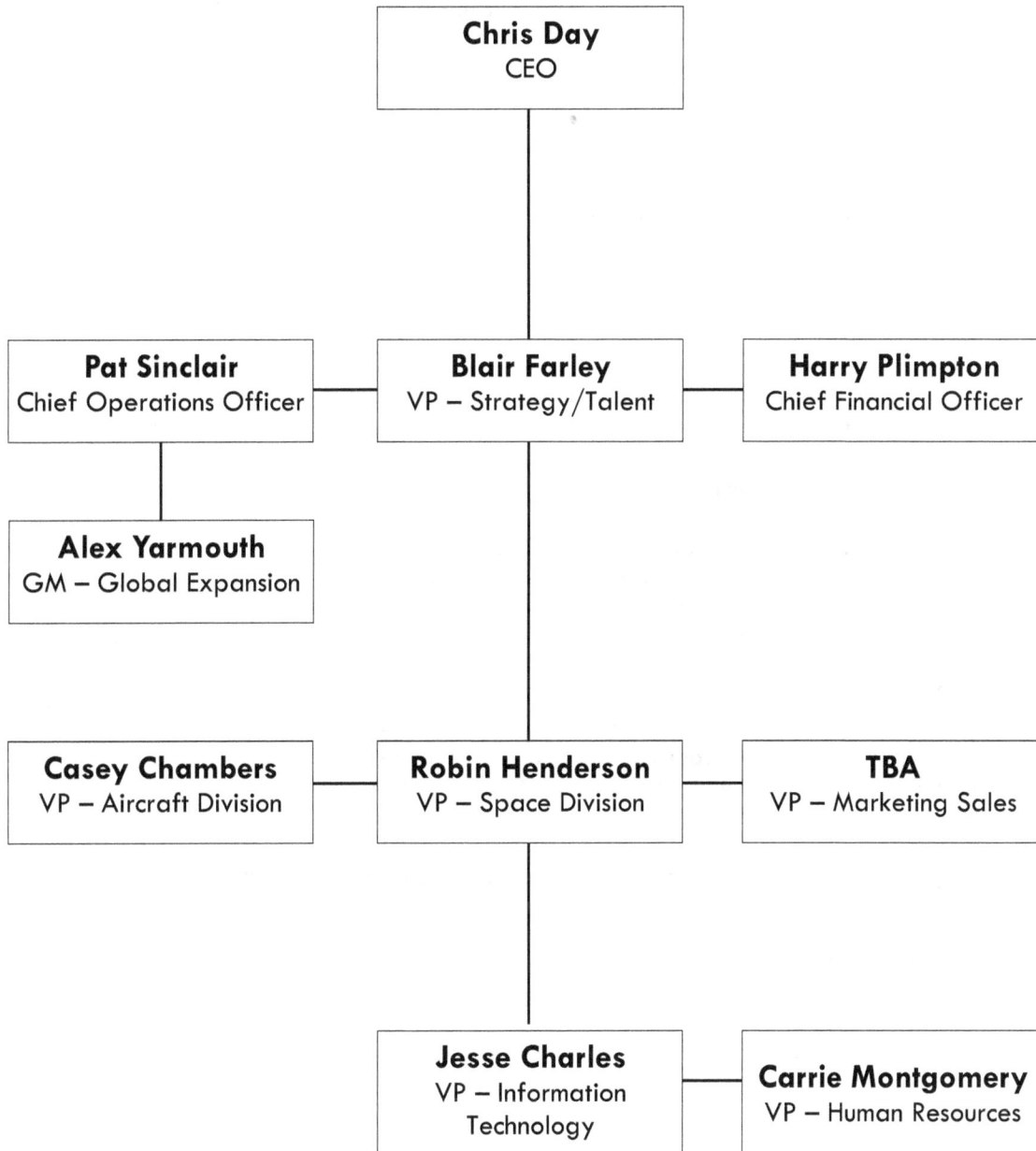

```
                    ┌─────────────────────┐
                    │     Chris Day       │
                    │        CEO          │
                    └─────────────────────┘
```

Pat Sinclair	Blair Farley	Harry Plimpton
Chief Operations Officer	VP – Strategy/Talent	Chief Financial Officer

Alex Yarmouth
GM – Global Expansion

Casey Chambers	Robin Henderson	TBA
VP – Aircraft Division	VP – Space Division	VP – Marketing Sales

Jesse Charles	Carrie Montgomery
VP – Information Technology	VP – Human Resources

BP2

Aerotech Briefing

Human Resources Team

HR at Aerotech is a centralized organization located out of the main facility in Houston. Over the last few years, the function has continued to shrink with budget cuts and workload and morale are issues within HR. The team is expected to set and monitor HR policy, deliver annual program support (i.e. Performance Appraisals) and manage all aspects of recruitment and hiring.

There is skeleton staff in other locations to handle local issues, and the European HR department is pretty much on its own, due to language and government legislation considerations in each country.

Issues:

- There is a real shortage of skilled technical expertise in the Aircraft side of the business. The Space program seems to attract a higher caliber of technical qualification and is perceived as the "future" of the company. In the past, attempts to cross-pollinate talent across both organizations have failed.

- Aerotech is an organization primarily made up of men (most with a military history). There is only 1 VP who is a woman (the VP of HR!) and minimal representation on the senior leadership team. Despite programs to grow technical and management skills for women, the percentage of women in Aerotech remains at 15%. Larry, the previous CEO was a "man's man" and surrounded himself with others like him.

- The expansion into Europe was a pet project of Larry's and it was pushed through very quickly (some calling it Larry's swan song). In general, there is a lack of understanding of the European environment and little communication exists between the two continents. This is actually a bit of a relief for the U.S. team, since they are busy enough with existing programs and processes.

- Carrie Montgomery is the VP of HR. With a marketing background, she has been keen to come up with some new programs for Aerotech. As usual, the Space division is more eager to adopt them, Aircraft more resistant. So, these new programs have only sporadic implementation, as each division and geo decides for themselves which they will adopt:

  o Revised Benefits Program, designed to allow employees to select which level of benefits coverage they need and share in some of the costs

  o New Skills Program which asks each employee to assess their skills annually and create a database of available skills

  o Management Training Program to identify high potential executive candidates and coach/mentor them with executives in other divisions

BP2

Aircraft Division Team

The Aircraft Division is and has always been the bread and butter of Aerotech. Not only is the manufacturing and production of large aircraft the oldest division of Aerotech, but also it makes up 60% of the revenue and most of Aerotech's profit. The cornerstones of the success of our division are long-standing relationships with large customers and suppliers, high product quality control standards and solid management practices.

Casey Chambers who heads up the Division, has been in his position for 15 years and was expected to be named as Larry's successor.

Issues:

- Casey has a no-nonsense, gruff and likeable style. He likes to get out and meet the folks on the floor, shake hands and ask about the families of employees but is still considered to be out-of-touch with real issues. Although he appears to invite new ideas (through suggestion boxes and at large group meetings), he prefers to make most decisions on his own, with the counsel of a small group of "in" advisors. This has been causing frustration with some of the newer professional hires who feel somewhat stifled.

- Retention of highly skilled technical employees (i.e. engineers) has been a problem over the last 5-8 years. Although there is recruitment on-campus and through regular programs, attrition has remained at a steady 12% - most within the first 3 years of employment. Some of these folks have been more attracted to the Space Program at Aerotech and have put in for transfers to the more progressive exciting area of the company. This has only added fuel to the existing rivalry between the two divisions.

- Because the Aircraft Division has been funding the investment (and some losses) in the Space Program, budget restrictions on the Aircraft Division seem too high, particularly since Aircraft provides most of Aerotech's profit. Many of the management team have expressed concern as to why productivity challenges continue to be issued to Aircraft but not the Space Division – it doesn't seem fair given Aircraft's ongoing and sustained contributions to Aerotech's success.

- Casey and the rest of the team do not understand the urgency for global expansion. With 12 sites in the U.S. and demonstrated leadership and customer satisfaction, it's unclear why more production is needed outside the U.S. borders. And the GM of Global Expansion seems to want to do things in his own way, without learning and using the sound practices developed in the States. Since inviting him for a tour of the flagship location in Houston, there has not been much communication.

BP2

Aerotech Briefing

Space Division Team

This is where all the action happens! Exploiting new technology, working with the greatest minds in the company (and the aerospace industry) and getting lots of Public Relations attention – the Space Division is the place to be! Founded in the early 70's, the Division has been involved in every major space mission in some capacity, and has large prominent contracts with NASA and the State Department. Although some of the projects have lost money, this is inevitable given some of the deadlines imposed by government customers and the high profile nature of the aerospace industry.

Robin Henderson is a brilliant PhD, and although only hired 8 years ago, has risen quickly to become the VP of the Space Division. Although considered somewhat of a loner amongst the Executive team, Robin is well respected within the Division and the management team welcomes the new ideas.

Issues:

- Despite a pilot program in partnership with the I/T Division, the e-commerce initiatives have not taken off as well as expected. The Space Division has wanted to participate in setting industry standards for electronic data interchange (EDI) working with a couple of large customers and the Department of Defense. Funding has been tight and cut back a few times, causing frustration with progress.

- There is definite friction between the "dot.com" mentality of the Space Division and the conservative, military approach of the rest of the company. It makes collaboration on common projects (i.e.: improved parts utilization) painfully slow, with personalities and hidden agendas clear but unresolved.

BP2

Finance Team

Finance is a well-run, traditional department within Aerotech. Although keeping good personnel has continued to be a minor concern (high overtime and stress at certain times of the year), for the most part, Finance has remained pretty much stable since the inception of Aerotech.

Issues:

- Both profit and revenue are down for 3 quarters in a row. Despite numerous meetings and reviews (backed up by filing cabinets worth of data), the situation continues to deteriorate.

- The Global Expansion team is slow in reporting quarterly financial results (partly due to technical difficulties with system compatibility). This makes it difficult to pull together a complete company picture.

- Overall company retention is a problem – 11% overall compared to an industry average of 9%.

BP2

Global Expansion Team

Global Expansion is a fairly new division in Aerotech, conceived only 3 years ago by then CEO Larry Banning. He felt that by truly creating a global corporation, not only could Aerotech capture share in other markets, but by having local manufacturing in geographies around the world – jobs would be created and tricky local legislation issues could be handled nearby. Not to mention new alliances with governments around the world. So, the dream was born!

After personally researching and visiting possible sites, Larry decided on investing in 3 new locations: Norway, Italy and Hong Kong. He then appointed Alex Yarmouth as the GM of the project, a solid performer with a Finance background who had done a tour of duty in Europe. The vision is to develop in at least 10 other sites across Europe and Asia/Australia over the next 5 years.

Issues:

- From the beginning, the expansion has been plagued with difficulties and delays. After his original interest, Larry has delegated all responsibility to Alex – while asking for frequent updates and progress reports. Although given a fairly generous initial budget, staffing has continued to plague Alex and a strong leader for the Hong Kong operation has not yet been found, which Alex continues to personally oversee. And working with local governments has been difficult at best, although the Italian team is doing well, having gotten off to a fast start by forging strong partnerships with the local government.

- The Aircraft Division who was to assist with the implementation has not proven to be very cooperative. No one executive was assigned to work with Alex and all attempts to get access to processes, policies and past history have been like pulling teeth. There was one half-hearted invitation to attend a briefing in Houston but it was more of a show-and-tell story than the working session that Alex envisioned. Despite the lack of information sharing, Alex has forged ahead with 3 splashy openings over the last 18 months.

- Alex feels that his status as a GM does not give him equal status with the rest of the Executive Committee who are all Vice-Presidents. He often gets left off important communications or meetings, and decisions are made without his input. On more than a few occasions, Alex has brought forward some innovative ideas that were conceived in his new role, but has always been shot down, with comments like "well, that may work in your territory, but not here." Most recently, he stumbled into a potentially global deal originating in Norway that would need participation from all geographies – it was met with lukewarm reception by the Committee. Larry was aware of Alex's concerns but urged him to focus on his own priorities for the time being.

BP2

Information Technology Team

I/T is proud of the incredibly complex and matrixed network of systems and applications it supports for such a large organization around the world. Many of the team's energies (and money) were dedicated to averting any possible Y2K crises over the last couple of years, so all other investments and changes were put on hold. Having gotten through Y2K without a hitch (but with a lot of overtime!), the I/T Division is now looking to re-invent itself to stay competitive, having provided overdue maintenance and support since Jan 1, 2000.

Issues:

- The global expansion has been a big part of the I/T team's focus in the recent months. Deciding on the right infrastructure, dealing with language and legal restrictions (not to mention time zones) has been challenging but rewarding. Unfortunately, system response time in the new sites has been an ongoing issue with lots of complaints. Also, there was an expectation that all new employees in the growing countries would be pc-literate which hasn't proven to be consistently true. The training solution for this problem is still under discussion.

- E-commerce is clearly the way to conduct business in the future (and recent past). The I/T Team has presented a number of white papers and business cases on how to implement across all divisions, to improve customer satisfaction and stay competitive. To date, only the Space Division has shown much interest and is working with I/T on a pilot program. The I/T team is frustrated with this lack of adoption and thinks that a key reason that Aerotech is losing profit and market share is this failure to move ahead.

- A nagging problem that has plagued Jesse Charles, VP of Information Technology for a number of years is the complete refusal of the Executive Committee to utilize personal technology. All were outfitted with state-of-the-art laptops, personalized one-on-one training sessions (most were never held) and direct support whenever needed. With the exception of 2 VP's (HR & Space Divisions), the machines have gathered dust and communication has continued to be via meetings, memos and through secretaries – slowing down decision-making and productivity substantially. Jesse tried to bring this issue forward to Larry once or twice, but since Larry was a prime offender, it was a touchy topic.

BP2

FIELD GUIDE

LEGACY
Leadership

THE REFERENCE GUIDE

ISBN # 0-9672175-2-0

Using the Field Guide

The contents of this guide are a concise and compact presentation of the Legacy Leadership® framework, and the comprehensive models contained within Legacy Leadership®. We have been asked by many people to make this Guide available for personal learning applications. We trust you will find the information here not only useful, but revolutionary in your approach to leadership.

This document is intended to be a reference guide, and for this reason does not read like a "book" on leadership. We have provided a brief **introduction to Legacy Leadership**®, followed by the **core concepts** of the model, the 5 Best Practices, utilizing tables, charts and bullet points. All of the material should be relatively self-explanatory. Each best practice is composed of three parts: the action descriptor, the BEING, and two DOING descriptors. For example, Best Practice #1 is Holder of Vision and Values™. HOLDER is the BEING part of this best practice, and the Vision and Values are the DOING part. The successful practice of each of these is dependent upon understanding each separate part to make the whole. Information given for each best practice includes Definitions, Critical Factors, Application, Legacy Steps, Language and *LegacyShifts*. There is also a summary page for each Best Practice included at the end of the material for each one, titled "Aerial View." The layout is designed for note taking should you desire to personalize your understanding of this unique leadership development framework.

Following the presentation of the Legacy Leadership® model and concepts, a blank **development plan** which can be completed by you, based upon your results from the Legacy Leadership® Competency Inventory™ (LLCI) is provided. You will need this inventory to complete this section. If you do not have the LLCI, these are available through the CoachWorks® webstore, www.CoachWorks.com. CoachWorks® also provides a full 360 Feedback online service based on this inventory.

If you have further questions about Legacy Leadership® or CoachWorks® International, Inc., we would enjoy hearing from you. Please visit our website, and contact us either through e-mail or voice mail with your comments and questions. We hope you will join the ranks of Legacy Leaders® spreading out across the corporate and organizational environment, the global marketplace and every other area where people want and need a framework for personal and professional excellence, for today and tomorrow.

Welcome to Legacy Leadership®.

The World Has Changed

Yes, it's true. **The world HAS changed,** especially the business world. Consider these shifts:

- "Command and Control" leadership does not work anymore.

- People expect more and different competencies from leaders today.

- Long term corporate loyalty is a thing of the past.

- Smart workers expect more reason for them to excel than producing profit for someone else.

- People today hold more positions, make more career shifts and handle more responsibilities than ever before.

- Global competition demands top talent, and leadership must attract and retain the best in the workforce.

- Workers expect leaders to be interested in them, not just the bottom line.

- Leaders must develop other leaders, build teams and foster collaborative cultures.

- Technology is unfolding so quickly that the maturing process for leadership development is short-circuited.

- Today's young executives have not had the opportunity to learn the vital people skills required for leadership.

A Linkage Survey* of 2000+ leaders showed that their Top 10 challenges are:

- Creating leaders at all levels
- Linking leadership with the strategic plan
- Designing effective leader development programs
- Identifying leadership competencies
- Finding the ROI on leadership development work
- Finding the ROI on coaching and mentoring programs
- Applying systems to leadership development
- Developing the high potential leaders
- Partnering with senior managers in development
- Developing personal leadership skills

*Presented at 2000 Linkage Leadership Development Conference by Linkage President

"A business periodical asked a number of corporate chief executives "to look over the horizon of today's headlines," "size up the future," and describe the most pressing tasks that lie beyond the millennium for chief executives. I was invited to do so as well. In my response I wrote, "The three major challenges CEOs will face have little to do with managing the enterprise's tangible assets and everything to do with monitoring the quality of: leadership, the workforce, and relationships."

Frances Hesselbein,
"The How To Be Leader."
Edited Book: The Leader of the Future:
New Visions, Strategies, and Practices for
the Next Era.
Jossey-Bass Publishers,
San Francisco, CA.

CoachWorks®' response is Legacy Leadership®.

Introduction to Legacy Leadership

What Is Legacy Leadership®?

Legacy Leadership® is the wisdom of the ages structured and packaged for today's - and tomorrow's - leaders. Its truths and Best Practices are timeless, proven keys to sustained significance—and form the foundation for real-time legacy in today's business environment. Legacy Leadership® is a complete program—a philosophy, a process, and a model. Legacy Leadership® is not a leadership style—it is a life system and a way of "being" not just "doing."

This vital and highly adaptable model was developed as the result of over 40 years of the combined experiences of the CoachWorks® principals in individual, corporate, and organizational leadership development. Legacy Leadership® is more than a program. The founders of CoachWorks® International have refined reliable time-honored principles into an intentional, powerful system for success—today and tomorrow. For self and for others.

Are you living your legacy? "Legacy" is commonly thought to be something you leave behind when you're gone. What if you were living your legacy now? What if your vision for the future was evident in everything you do, every day? It can happen.

Drs. Lee Smith and Jeannine Sandstrom developed the Legacy Leadership® program as a result of their work with business leaders in all sectors. When they observed the most common behaviors of successful leaders, they identified the Best Practices that set outstanding leaders apart from their peers. When they listened to the deepest issues that were on leaders' minds, they were matters of legacy. The Legacy Leadership® program was developed as a map for ensuring excellence in leadership practices that would enable leaders to leave the legacy they intended.

CoachWorks® International has isolated, defined, and made transferable the practices common to leaders who are able to achieve and sustain success—with people, product, and revenue. Legacy Leadership® is based on 5 Best Practices which are common in all great leaders, whether it be the ancients whose successes leap from the worn pages of history, or the Fortune 500 leaders of today—and will be observed in the leaders of tomorrow.

Legacy Leadership® is a philosophy, a model, and a proven process for bringing out individual best, developing other leaders in the organization, establishing organizational leadership culture, and positively impacting the bottom line.

Current leader books and articles cover various aspects and techniques of leadership, but do not deliver a comprehensive model. Legacy Leadership® is a complete framework of practices, behaviors, attitudes and values that addresses every aspect of successful leadership.

Legacy Leaders® become students of leadership while focusing on building other leaders who build leaders, who build leaders...

We hear stories every day about the lack of strong leadership talent. Legacy Leadership® is a comprehensive model for developing such talented leaders. It includes competencies and practices with immediate applicability to most every possibility and challenge leaders face today. These practices embrace both vision and accountability for results, as well as methods for creating an environment for team success, strong and dependable relationships, and maximizing the talents of diverse perspectives and strengths.

Introduction to Legacy Leadership

Many organizations have a set of competencies with which to measure their leader performance; others do not. In either case, Legacy Leadership® provides a sound structure for such competencies to reside. With the structural map of the 5 Best Practices, you have a full and complete picture of the destination your leader development program will go, for you personally, and for those you lead. The basic focus of Legacy Leadership® is on OTHERS, rather than on the leader, in order to develop leaders who then develop other leaders. The outcome is fully developed leaders, both current and emerging, and a greatly enhanced leadership potential within the organization.

Legacy, in this model, is not about building things, but building people. It is about investing in individual leaders who then share what they have learned with others. Legacy is realized in this perpetuating cycle of leadership development by enabling your personal and organizational plan to come alive and thrive. Your best self is offered to others in order to develop their best selves and so on, leaving a multi-generational imprint—a living legacy.

Leadership Competencies and Critical Success Skills—
The 5 Best Practices of Legacy Leadership®

Given that leadership can be complex, we have simplified and distinguished five core competency platforms and associated critical success skills for successful leadership. These platforms represent a complete set of observable and measurable behaviors. The behaviors, when used in total, are leverage points for success. We have included those practices of leadership that are essential for every leader, regardless of their industry or level within the organization.

There are many leaders in our world, but only those who desire to grow their competencies will be the most successful, influential and effective leaders; and more importantly, leaders whom people desire to follow—*Legacy Leaders*®.

Now, like no other time in history, there is a need to develop strong leadership abilities. Using a model with proven success for both the best of times and worst of times, Legacy Leadership® embodies a compelling and comprehensive set of competencies and skills. Legacy Leaders® lead the way for others to follow to the edge of current development and beyond.

Legacy Leadership® is:

- A complete leadership program, addressing every aspect of successful leadership
- A plan that changes the culture of an organization from a command post to a community
- A method to actively grow tomorrow's leaders...today
- A hands-on, hands-together commitment to meeting mutual goals
- A set of practices to inspire and develop positive changes within any organization or individual
- A philosophy of leadership that encourages confidence, learning, wisdom, courage, insight and compassion
- A process to achieve personal best, team best and company best
- A framework of practices, behaviors, attitudes and values that energizes people and their organizations
- A balanced approach to people and production
- A way to reach great potential and possibilities
- A way to attract and retain high potential employees of diverse perspectives
- Simple, yet powerful. It works.

Introduction to Legacy Leadership

Readiness Indicators

Legacy Leadership® provides a complete structure and framework around which both individuals and whole organizations can become Legacy Leaders®—nurturing, promoting and influencing not only today's leaders, but growing tomorrow's as well.

LEGACY LEADERSHIP® is a comprehensive model for ***individual professionals*** who:

- want to work within a congruent and consistent leadership system that is well-structured for insuring organizational success.
- want a method for holding themselves and others accountable for success.
- want to develop personal creativity and become more innovative and flexible.
- would like to be able to see change as a great opportunity and to envision new possibilities with other members of their team.
- would like to become more of a mentor, modeling leadership practices and attitudes to others in their team.
- would like to stretch to become the very best they can be in all areas of life, both professionally and personally.
- want to inspire others, and be inspired, to see and reach the greatest potentials.
- want work to be fun, and also promote that environment for others.
- are ready to change attitudes, break out of old habits and create new successes.
- are willing to make an investment in time and commitment for themselves, and the Company.

LEGACY LEADERSHIP® serves as a leadership development tool for ***companies and organizations*** that:

- want leadership that sets a clear direction.
- desire an organization-wide leadership standard.
- would like a reputation in the outside corporate world of integrity and employee value.
- want to attract and retain high potential employees.
- would like to be sure the right people are in the right positions for optimum efficiency and output.
- want to increase loyalty among customers.
- want to be known as "the place to work" in the marketplace of talent.
- want higher performance and more measurable outcomes.
- want a healthier bottom line.
- are willing to expand out from old boundaries and learn new patterns for success.
- are willing to make an investment in the future of its employees, its purpose, and its financial goals.

Legacy Leadership® makes it easy to embrace a powerful leadership system throughout an organization by providing the guidelines and simple framework for individuals to sustain that culture. Legacy Leadership® was designed for leadership development—at all levels both professionally and organizationally. Every employee is a potential leader, capable of becoming a true *Legacy Leader*®.

LEGACY LEADERSHIP® outlines and defines the way the organization does business—in every meeting, every operation, every project, every level.

Notes

Introduction to Legacy Leadership

The Legacy Leadership® Logo

In this introduction to Legacy Leadership®, the logo is seen in black and white only, in 5 square blocks:

It is obviously representative of the 5 Best Practices. However, the original logo is designed in color (as seen on the back cover of this book) and the colors have meaning which may be helpful in recalling the 5 Best Practices. We thought we would share that information with you here.

We are often asked about the colors used in the Legacy Leadership® logo and model. Do they have significance? We wanted bright, bold, crisp and clean colors for this leadership model—well defined, highly visible and not muted—just like our leadership and our legacy should be. That was the primary motivator for selecting the colors found here. The colors were also identified with each of the 5 Best Practices in order to provide some easily remembered association.

Yellow, bright and "sunny," is often associated with light and vision. **Yellow is the color of Best Practice 1: Holder of Vision and Values**™. The Legacy Leader® holds and sustains the vision, aligning it with values (personally, professionally, and organizationally). Without this "light," goals remain in the dark. The Legacy Leader® carries the light of vision everywhere. This Best Practice is about direction and commitment.

Blue is the color of cloudless skies. It reminds us of great expanses, unlimited horizons and rich opportunities. For this reason, **blue has been assigned to Best Practice 2: Creator of Collaboration and Innovation**™. A creator brings something into being through original and inventive means. A Legacy Leader® creates collaboration and innovation, painting a wide and limitless picture of new possibilities—the sky is the limit. This Best Practice is about creating a positive environment for working relationships.

Red is the color of the heart. It is associated with the very core and being of something, and thus it has been **linked with Best Practice 3: Influencer of Inspiration and Leadership**™. This Best Practice is the heart of Legacy Leadership®. The Legacy Leader® influences, inspires and models excellence in leadership for everyone. This Best Practice is about making connections with individuals—the heart of relationships as well as leadership.

Green is the color of growth. Personal, professional and organizational growth is stimulated by drawing upon the strengths of others, which is the intent of **Best Practice 4: Advocator of Differences and Community**™. The Legacy Leader® intentionally recognizes differences as potential strengths and community growth stimulators. This Best Practice is about distinguishing individual strengths and inclusion of differing perspectives into one community.

Purple is a color often associated with royalty, and royalty can imply authority—and accountability. A king's subjects are called upon to give account for their service under him. They are responsible to him. **Purple has been assigned to Best Practice 5: Calibrator of Responsibility and Accountability**™. We believe this is a noble Best Practice, and one most often misunderstood and neglected! This Best Practice is about execution and performance measured against vision and values.

We hope these colors will help bring the 5 Best Practices to mind for easy remembrance, and serve as a quick and efficient template for leadership behavior.

1

Holder of Vision And Values™

About direction and commitment

2

Creator of Collaboration and Innovation™

About the environment of working relationships

3

Influencer of Inspiration and Leadership™

About connecting with individuals, the heart of relationships

4

Advocator of Differences and Community™

About distinction and inclusion

LEGACY Leadership®

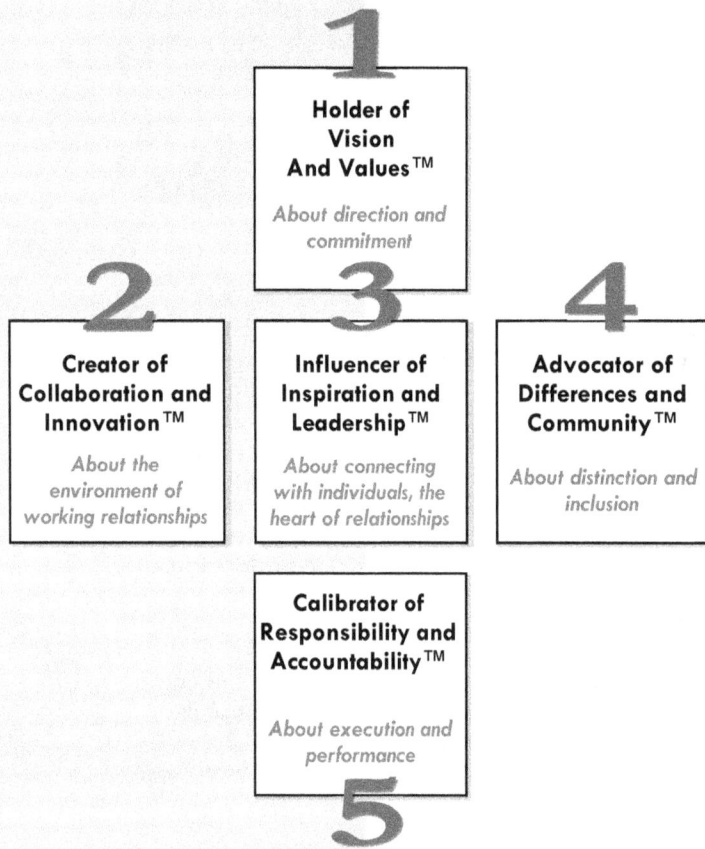

Legacy Leadership® is based upon 5 core competency platforms for successful leadership which we call The 5 Best Practices. Most major leadership models or approaches will find a fit within this balanced framework. We have included those practices of leadership that are essential for every leader, regardless of their industry or level within the organization.

These practice areas form the context of the Legacy Leadership® Model. For each Best Practice there are 10 Critical Success Skills which detail the basic skills, competencies, behaviors and attitudes within this model. These are summarized briefly in the table below.

Calibrator of Responsibility and Accountability™

About execution and performance

5

The 5 Best Practices

Holder of Vision and Values™	Creator of Collaboration and Innovation™	Influencer of Inspiration and Leadership™	Advocator of Differences and Community™	Calibrator of Responsibility and Accountability™
ATTITUDE, BEHAVIOR or COMPETENCY	*ATTITUDE, BEHAVIOR or COMPETENCY*	*ATTITUDE, BEHAVIOR or COMPETENCY*	*ATTITUDE, BEHAVIOR or COMPETENCY*	*ATTITUDE, BEHAVIOR or COMPETENCY*
1. Reinforce vision and values 2. Model principles 3. Integrate vision 4. Have strategic plan 5. Team alignment 6. Established measureables 7. Integrate values 8. Personal values 9. Desire to develop others 10. Communicate, sustain processes	1. Create innovative possibilities 2. Trusting environment 3. Masterful listener 4. Comfortable learning from others 5. Opportunities in disagreement 6. Timely questioning 7. Innovate now for future 8. Organizational and marketplace projection 9. Discern need (or not) for change 10. Facilitate best group thinking	1. Develop relationships 2. Emotional intelligence and positive energy to influence others 3. Model positive perspective 4. Evoke best in others 5. Acknowledge contributions 6. Delegate for development 7. Showcase others 8. Inspiring risk taker 9. Minimize negative impact of decisions 10. Achieve through others with humility, resolve	1. Ready advocate 2. Mentor for visibility 3. Strengths-based culture 4. Connoisseur of talent 5. Team diversity 6. Cross-functional opportunities 7. Inter-departmental collaboration 8. Greater community thinking 9. Internal-External communication 10. United inclusive environment	1. Strategic plan with checks + balances 2. Know milestone status 3. Team clear about responsibilities 4. Require peak performance/support with resources 5. Feedback and appropriate action 6. Personal, organizational accountabilities 7. Action plan with provision for adjustments 8. Urgency in achievement, change 9. Alert to trends, recalibrate 10. Team commitment, appropriate consequences
1	**2**	**3**	**4**	**5**

Introduction to Legacy Leadership

Definitions

DEFINITIONS			EXPLANATION
Holder of Vision and Values™			**1**
HOLDER	**VISION**	**VALUES**	This Best Practice is about direction and commitment. The term "holder" indicates that the leader lives the vision and values while measuring every action against both. The leader then provides consistent focus and direction. The critical success skills include: integration of vision/values into all responsibilities, having a well-defined strategic plan, team translation of vision and values, establishing milestones and benchmarks, modeling the practice, developing the potential of others to pull out the best in them, and effectively communicating and sustaining organizational vision/values.
One who "keeps" in hand those things that are important, by embracing and encouraging their remembrance.	A clear view and understanding of realizable goals, plans and intentions.	Those things considered right, worthwhile and desirable—the basis of guiding principles and standards.	
Creator of Collaboration and Innovation™			**2**
CREATOR	**COLLABORATION**	**INNOVATION**	This Best Practice is about creating a positive environment for working relationships. The term "creator" indicates the leader's ability to create a learning trusting environment where collaboration and innovation can occur. The critical success skills include abilities to: unleash innovation, listen masterfully, learn from others, be aware of the bigger picture, discern when change needs to occur, and being a masterful facilitator.
One who causes something to "come into being" through original or inventive means.	The process of working together to achieve common goals instead of personal agenda.	The introduction of something new and different to the process of achieving goals	
Influencer of Inspiration and Leadership™			**3**
INFLUENCER	**INSPIRATION**	**LEADERSHIP**	This Best Practice is about making connections with individuals—the heart of relationships as well as leadership. The term "influencer" indicates the leader's ability to influence and inspire for positive relationships. The critical success skills include abilities to: influence positively, demonstrate high levels of emotional intelligence, bring out the best in people by developing them fully, focus on others rather than self, make tough decisions with minimal people impact, and be humble while holding resolve to accomplish stated goals.
One who brings about a desired effect in others, by direct or indirect means.	The process of animating, motivating or encouraging others to reach new levels of achievement.	The process of guiding and directing others to shared success.	
Advocator of Differences and Community™			**4**
ADVOCATOR	**DIFFERENCES**	**COMMUNITY**	This Best Practice is about distinguishing individual strengths and inclusion of differing perspectives. The term "advocator" indicates the leader's ability to support and stand for strengths-based talent. The critical success skills include abilities to: be an advocator of individuals, be a connoisseur of talent, insist on teams with diverse perspectives and abilities, stand for cross-functional development and collaboration, recognize community impact, and promote an inclusive environment united toward a common focus.
One who stands in support of a cause, a practice or a person on its or their behalf.	Those qualities that distinguish people or things from other people or things.	A group of people with shared interest working together to achieve shared success.	
Calibrator of Responsibility and Accountability™			**5**
CALIBRATOR	**RESPONSIBILITY**	**ACCOUNTABILITY**	This Best Practice is about execution and performance measured against vision and values. The term "calibrator" indicates constant vigilance, with possible adjustments, of progress toward accomplishing responsibilities and accountabilities. The critical success skills include abilities to: execute successfully, maintain a "finger on the pulse" for status measurement, require peak performance, provide feedback and coaching, have clearly defined action plans, model a sense of urgency in getting things done and respond to change, be alert to trends, and gain commitment to follow-through.
One who "sets the mark" for the quantitative measurement of success/acceptance.	The ability to respond correctly to—and meet—stated expectations.	The obligation to justify conduct, conditions or circumstances.	

Introduction to Legacy Leadership

The 5 Best Practices: Being and Doing

Each of the 5 Best Practices has three components: one part BEING, and two parts DOING. Most leadership models have a list of competencies, skills and actions that contribute to good leadership. But great leaders don't just DO, they ARE. As we initially sought to label the 5 Best Practices, it became difficult to apply a simple label to include all the inherent components. We finally settled on labels that actually said what was meant, and were not merely coined terms or jargon. Too often people focus merely on the doing of leadership. It is vital to consider BOTH aspects of being and doing. BEING involves a certain consciousness, awareness of who the leader is.

Best Practice 1: HOLDER OF VISION AND VALUES™
BEING: Holder

Great leaders are conscious guardians of both personal and organizational vision and values. It becomes part of who they are, and guides all they do. BEING a Holder implies understanding the necessity of never allowing vision and values to slip out of focus or priority. Merely having vision, or having values is not enough. They must be intentionally held. A Legacy Leader® is very clear about his or her own personal core vision and values, which are the driving forces for their leadership. Leadership is not just about doing vision, and doing values—professionally or organizationally. A Legacy Leader® LIVES them, preserves them, and relies upon them as a guide.

Best Practice 2: CREATOR of COLLABORATION and INNOVATION™
BEING: Creator

Collaboration and Innovation don't happen by themselves. They must be encouraged, nurtured, with opportunities created by leaders. This is not about being <u>creative</u>, it is about being a <u>creator</u>, one who instinctively creates opportunities where collaboration and innovation can flourish. A creator actually causes something to come into being, in this case collaboration and innovation, sometimes through inventive means. The Legacy Leader® becomes an active "opportunity seeker" and possibility thinker. This is an attitude of leadership, not just a leadership action.

Best Practice 3: INFLUENCER of INSPIRATION AND LEADERSHIP™
BEING: Influencer

A Legacy Leader® understands that we cannot NOT influence, and therefore becomes an intentional influencer. It is about having a consciousness that all that we do influences, even when we aren't aware of it. In all we do, we will either influence in a positive or negative way. The Legacy Leader® makes a choice to BE an influencer in a positive way, regardless of the situation or circumstances. This becomes a way of life, a way of being. This awareness tempers our behavior both personally and professionally.

(continued...)

Introduction to Legacy Leadership

The 5 Best Practices: Being and Doing

(continued)

Best Practice 4: **ADVOCATOR of DIFFERENCES and COMMUNITY**™
BEING: Advocator
An advocator is one who stands firm in support. It is about BEING someone who is courageous enough to take a stand, and stay standing. It means having a well-defined sense of right, and the internal strength to defend it. A leader cannot DO this, if he or she cannot BE it. It is an unfortunate truth in business today that we do not find too many people who are so clear about who they are that they are willing to take a firm stand regardless of consequences. But a Legacy Leader® is a ready advocate for what is right, which often involves risk. The word advocator was selected because it carries more strength than defender or supporter. This is about internal commitment to causes, practices and people.

Best Practice 5: **CALIBRATOR of RESPONSIBILITY and ACCOUNTABILITY**™
BEING: Calibrator
A calibrator is one who is clear about standards, vision, values, and what is right both personally and organizationally, and measures all behavior against them. This is an ongoing internal process that never stops. It is a natural, conscious and continual setting of the "mark" and adjusting what is necessary to hit it consistently. It implies a sense of awareness, measurement and appropriate adjustment. Again, it is not just doing, it is being vigilant, accountable, responsible, thoughtful and nimble, with a constant eye on the target. A Legacy Leader® is a human thermostat, always measuring the environment and adjusting as necessary.

Legacy Shifts

As leaders transition into Legacy Leaders®, they will be making shifts from ordinary to extraordinary leadership skills and competencies. We call these Legacy *Shifts*™:

- FROM Leaving a Legacy **TO LIVING A LEGACY**
- FROM Financial focus **TO PEOPLE FOCUS**
- FROM Knowing it all **TO LIFE-LONG LEARNING**
- FROM Focus on self **TO FOCUS ON OTHERS**
- FROM Exclusion **TO INCLUSION**
- FROM Labeling **TO HONORING**
- FROM Knowledge for personal power
  TO KNOWLEDGE FOR POWERFUL ORGANIZATIONS
- FROM Rules **TO GUIDING PRINCIPLES**
- FROM Jargon **TO CLEAR LANGUAGE**
- FROM Allowing Exceptions **TO NO EXCEPTIONS** (not even for me)

Introduction to Legacy Leadership

The Essence

BEST PRACTICE	Holder of Vision and Values™ 1	Creator of Collaboration and Innovation™ 2	Influencer of Leadership and Inspiration™ 3	Advocator of Differences and Community™ 4	Calibrator of Responsibility and Accountability™ 5
DESCRIPTION	Leaders embody, hold out for all to know, company's vision and values. Vision and values spell out where company is going and the guiding principles by which they will operate. Leaders' behaviors are such that all work is organized around these 2 factors and leadership team, all performance measured against them.	Leaders supply environments where team members are comfortable enough to create possibilities greater than they would have alone. The group then discovers new practices, tool or products that changes or improves everything.	Leaders are "trail blazers" with a positive influence so that everyone is lifted up to be the best they can be. Participants are invited (not commanded) to contribute from strengths and are filled with energy to deliver high quality outcomes.	Leaders possess a mindset that all people have unique and compelling contributions to make. Leaders speak up for each person to forward that person's development and progress with the company.	Leaders who demonstrate personal standards of behavior and accountability, who provide clarity about expectations for results and who ensure measurement of progress toward the vision, with an eye for flexibility and mid-course corrections.
CRITICAL FACTORS	**Must be in place:** • Clear, compelling vision • Values statement • Business objectives • Strategic design • Roadmap and milestones • Communication throughout company of all above • Ways to measure all	**Must be in place:** • Creative environment • Commitment to innovation • Processes for collaboration • High levels of trust • Process of capturing outcomes	**Must be in place:** • Positively inspired leaders • Abilities and processes to engage others from strengths • Personal connections • Stories that inspire	**Must be in place:** • Processes for identifying strengths and styles • Comfort with differing perspectives • Practice inclusion vs exclusion	**Must be in place:** • Calibration processes vs discipline • Measurements and rewards • Measurements against roadmap and milestones
BARRIERS TO SUCCESS	**What prevents** • **success?** • Lack of commitment • Missing Communication • Lack of Measurements • Focus on short term activity vs long term commitment • Lack of modeling of values by leadership	**What prevents success?** • Mindset for change avoidance • Lack of trust • Lack of inspiration by leader • Lack of methods for discovery • Fear of creative tension	**What prevents success?** • Focus on numbers not people • Not knowing what influences • Fear or mistrust • Previous history with the influencer	**What prevents success?** • Belief systems and biases • Stereotyping • "Rubber stamp" mentality • Avoidance of vulnerability • "Us against them" thinking	**What prevents success?** • Leader not holding self or others accountable • "Either/Or" thinking • Qualifiers that diminish • Exclusion of customer in the measurement mix

Introduction to Legacy Leadership
Expected Outcomes

BEST PRACTICE			ORGANIZATIONAL (Your Company)	PROFESSIONAL (Your Leader)
1	HOLDER	VISION	■ Clarity of focus ■ Strategic implementation against vision ■ Consistent communication about focus	■ Reminds people of what's important ■ Clear alignment with followers ■ Brings whole self to leadership
		VALUES	■ Reputation of a company with values ■ Congruent guiding principles in the culture ■ A culture of integrity	■ "Walks the Talk" of personal core values ■ Has meaning and purpose for efforts ■ Models authenticity
2	CREATOR	COLLABORATION	■ Fosters environment of trust and loyalty ■ Breaks down "silos" ■ Creates flexibility and adaptability	■ Puts ego aside to hear brilliance of others ■ Builds teams and networks ■ Brings out best, asks tough questions
		INNOVATION	■ Creative energy for competitive advantage ■ Fast learning ■ Environment of thought leadership	■ Enhanced personal creativity ■ Ability to shift quickly, personal agility ■ Embrace change as opportunity
3	INFLUENCER	INSPIRATION	■ Highly motivating environment ■ Encouragement to bring whole self to work ■ Employees feel valued for contribution	■ Is both inspired and inspiring ■ Passionate with focused energy ■ Models that work is FUN
		LEADERSHIP	■ Develops emerging leaders at all levels ■ Links leadership with strategic plan ■ A systems focus on leadership practices	■ Stretches to be the best ■ Leader competencies developed ■ Has a "platform" for actively mentoring
4	ADVOCATOR	DIFFERENCES	■ Is a "connoisseur" of talent ■ Taps abilities of ALL, including "fringes" ■ Reduced turnover, greater retention	■ Discovery of own uniqueness ■ Finds own distinguishing strength set ■ Learns from those who are different
		COMMUNITY	■ Reputation attractive to employees ■ Greater commitment to community ■ Greater sense of authentic purpose	■ Gets voice heard while hearing others ■ Releases old biases, is inclusive ■ Makes alliances between leader and led
5	CALIBRATOR	RESPONSIBILITY	■ Right people in right jobs ■ Optimized strengths ■ Consistent standards	■ Is the right leader for the job ■ Produces excellent results, value added ■ Requires everyone's personal responsibility
		ACCOUNTABILITY	■ High level of achievement ■ Measurable outcomes ■ Loyal customers	■ Holds self and others accountable ■ Communicates expectations ■ Calibrates regularly and consistently

Introduction to Legacy Leadership

Comparison Chart

LEADERSHIP MODEL	ORGANIZATION, PROFESSIONAL, OR BOTH	FOCUS	GOAL	Vision	Values	Collaboration	Innovation	Inspiration	Influence	Differences	Community	Responsibility	Accountability
Smith/ Sandstrom: Legacy Leadership	Both individual and organization	The "who" of the leader and the "what" of behavior. Based on a comprehensive set of 5 Best Practices: 1. Holder of Vision and Values™ 2. Creator of Collaboration and Innovation™ 3. Influencer of Inspiration and Leadership™ 4. Advocate of Differences and Community™ 5. Calibrator of Responsibility and Accountability™	To create a multiplication effect where leaders develop leaders, who develop leaders, who possess strength and agility to direct the organization to high levels of competition, profitability, and commitment to service of others.	X	X	X	X	X	X	X	X	X	X
Kouzes/ Posner: The Leadership Challenge	Individual development as he/she impacts the organization	Leader abilities: 1. Challenge the process 2. Inspire shared vision 3. Enable others to act 4. Model the way 5. Encourage the heart	To develop behaviors to serve as a basis for learning to lead.	X	X	X	X	X	X	X		X	
Covey: Principle-Centered Leadership	Individual leaders	Principles on which to base leadership: 1. Alignment 2. Empowerment 3. Trust 4. Trustworthiness	To practice leadership from perspective of 4 "true north" principles.	X	X				X			X	
Nanus: Visionary Leadership	Individual leaders	Helping to develop the right vision.	Guidance for leaders to develop vision and strategy	X	X								
Greenleaf: Servant Leadership	Individual leaders	On the being of the leader and his/her highest priority of serving others.	To serve first, lead second	X	X			X			X	X	
Ball: DNA Leadership	Individual leaders and organization	Goals are the transforming agent that creates a DNA culture.	Using DNA fabric for guiding and growing the Goal-Driven organization.	X	X			X	X				
Oakley/ Krug: Enlightened Leadership	Both leaders and organization	Right vision while leading organization members to accept ownership for it and commitment to implement vision	To inspire others to act, and developing other leaders.	X					X			X	
Blanchard: Situational Leadership	Individual professional	Leadership style people need to be successful at what they are doing—Three stages of change based on situational need: • Starting and orienting the journey • Change and Discouragement • Adopting and Refining Empowerment	Re-orients leader style based on evaluation of situation. Focuses on diagnosis, flexibility and partnering.	X	X	X				X		X	X

Managers or Leaders?

Distinctions Between Management and Leadership
The Importance of Each

NOTE: In order to truly understand the concepts embraced by Legacy Leadership, it is vital to understand first the distinctions between a manager and a leader. Leaders exalt differences and use them to build strong community, not merely manage them for production purposes.

Strong management systems have developed over the past 100 years. As our business world changes for the next century, there are different requirements for both management and leadership. Research[1] shows that there is a lack of available leadership at a time when forward thinking ability and creativity is needed in order to compete.

Many managers see the need and feel the desire to develop a personal shift from management to leadership in order for their companies to create and maintain a competitive edge. To produce such a paradigm shift, one must understand the distinctions between the two positions and follow through with appropriate action until automatically behaving as a leader.

Managers can and must make a shift to become leaders. Leaders can then shift further to a model of Legacy Leadership that builds legacy within people, teams and organizations [2].

(1) Kotter, John. 1990. A Force For Change: How Leadership Differs From Management
(2) Smith, Ritcheske and Sandstrom, 1999. Legacy Leadership: Five Best Practices

Managers or Leaders?

MANAGERS	LEADERS
Primary Activities of the Manager: - Plans and budgets - Organizes and staffs - Controls and solves problems - Maintains status quo - Produces outcomes while maintaining quality	**Primary Activities of the Leader:** - Establishes direction and creates vision and strategies - Aligns people around the vision - Motivates and inspires to reach the vision - Moves forward - Produces change
Language of the Manager: Has more directive statements and questions: - *"Let's create a method for getting this done in 45 days.* - *"We need staff to handle the new acquisition."* - *"Here's how we will control spending."* - *"What policies and procedures are needed?"* - *"This is how we will monitor implementation."* **Management Language addresses the WHO and HOW** - *"Let's organize to make this more effective."* - *"We will set up a system to measure results."* - *"What will it cost us?"* - *"What is expected of this plan?"* - *"Who do we need in terms of staff?"*	**Language of the Leader:** Asks more questions for discovery of possibilities: - *"What's being done now and what will we do in the future?"* - *"How does this align with moving toward our vision?"* - *"How can we support you as you move forward?"* - *"How will you measure results toward vision?* **Leader Language addresses the WHAT, WHEN and WHY** - *"What our customers (or competitors) think is….."* - *"When we focus on this agenda we will be closer to surpassing our original goals."* - *"What will it take to get people on board with this?"* - *"What are the risks and ramifications?"*
Focus of the Manager - Results - Organization - Plans - Numbers - Day to Day, Month to Month	**Focus of the Leader** - Development of people - Trends - Customer's needs - Strategy - Year to Year and Future

Similarities for both Management and Leadership:
- Both Management and Leadership are **complete implementation systems.**
    - Implementation for Management is production of consistent results by being on time and on budget.
    - Implementation for Leadership is aligning people to new directions and inspiring them to make it happen.
- Both decide what needs to be done.
- Both create networks of people and relationships that can accomplish an agenda.
- Both ensure that those people actually get the job done.

Notes

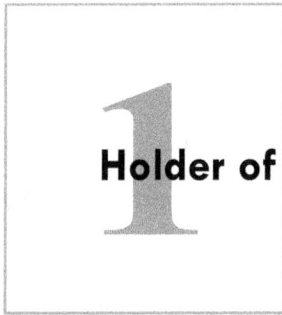

1 Holder of Vision and Values™

Holder of Vision and Values™

Basic Definitions

Holder

A HOLDER "keeps in hand" those things that are important, embracing and encouraging their remembrance.

Vision

VISION is a clear view and understanding of realizable goals, plans and intentions.

Values

VALUES are those things considered right, worthwhile, and desirable – the basis of guiding principles and standards.

Legacy Leadership® Definitions

The Legacy Leader will hold vision and values by:

- being clear on personal and organizational vision, guiding principles and standards and by measuring all ideas, decisions, commitment and actions against the organization's vision template and values template.

- encouraging, promoting and protecting organizational vision and values by embracing and encouraging their remembrance.

- establishing and maintaining this vision and values "holding" so that they become foundational to all activities.

The importance of values cannot be understated.
Values and beliefs drive human behavior.

Personal values and organizational values must match—
or the employee and the employer do not match.

Values drive our guiding principles around which we work with employees,
customers, vendors, and the community.

1

Holding **VISION**	*Holding* **VALUES**
Holding Vision is NOT:	**Holding Values is NOT:**
■ **Vague references to non-measurable goals** The organizational vision held by a Legacy Leader® is <u>NOT</u> giving vague references to "pie-in-the-sky" goals. This vision is concrete, measurable, and extendable to all organizational operations. Leadership has pre-established this clear and concise vision for a measuring guide throughout the organization.	■ **Enforcing "rules"** The organizational values held by a Legacy Leader® are <u>NOT</u> a set of arbitrary rules and regulations used to keep behavior in compliance. These values are the underpinning of the organization's business ethic, and are, in combination with vision, what drive every decision, process and activity. All such activity is measured against these values.
■ **A ruler to "slap hands"** The organization's vision held by Legacy Leadership® is <u>NOT</u> the proverbial "back of the hand" ruler of punishment or chastisement for failures to meet the vision. This vision is to be used daily in routine operation for measurement, for planning, for decision-making, and targeting.	■ **Merely acknowledging a behavior code** The organization's values held by a Legacy Leader® is <u>NOT</u> lip service to a behavior code, but rather wholehearted support of an overall ethical standard, including such things as integrity, respect and trust. This requires incorporation of these standards into every activity.
■ **Harboring "Secret Information"** The organizational vision held by a Legacy Leader® is <u>NOT</u> secret information to be guarded and kept secure. Holding this vision means communicating it often and well, incorporating it into daily operations, ensuring it becomes part of every employee's thinking process and measuring tool.	■ **Self Righteousness** The organizational and personal values held by a Legacy Leader® are <u>NOT</u> an excuse for self-righteous, arrogant and self-serving behavior. These values create the reputation of both organization and individual and are a reflection of the person and the company, establishing reputation and worth. The holding and promoting of these values precludes self righteous and self-serving behavior.

Critical Factors

1	*Holding* **VISION**	*Holding* **VALUES**
Factors for Success	■ Clear compelling organizational vision in writing ■ Excellent communication of vision throughout organization ■ Ways to measure vision ■ Roadmap and milestones ■ Compelling strategic design throughout organization ■ Knowledge of personal vision and match to organizational vision	■ Fully developed values statement and guiding principles that are clearly defined ■ Organization-wide communication of values ■ Measurement methods ■ Employee clarity and acceptance of values ■ Attitude of values underlying all work
Challenges (Potential Barriers)	■ No existing written or communicated organizational vision (goals are not stated, or not clearly communicated) ■ Teammates are not invested or interested in organizational vision — are self interested ■ Existing vision is not compelling, inspiring ■ Existing vision is not measurable	■ No existing established organizational values, guiding principles (not stated, or not clearly communicated) ■ Leadership does not model values ■ Individual "renegades" as exception to expected values-driven behavior ■ Existing values not "owned" by employees ■ Individuals with conflicting personal values

Vision is where the leader operates.

**Managers live in today.
Leaders live in the future.**

Application

1	Holding **VISION**	Holding **VALUES**
Behaviors and Competencies	**A Holder of Vision:** ■ has a well-defined personal vision. ■ clearly understands their organization's vision and uses it as a foundational purpose for all efforts. ■ has clear alignment with organization's vision, and its relationship with all individuals, teams, and activities. ■ brings his or her whole self to this leadership model. ■ consistently communicates, and strategizes around, and measures performance against the established organizational vision. ■ encourages others to create their own vision. ■ protects the vision from being diminished. ■ provides consistent focus and direction. ■ makes vision exciting, and helps it come alive in everyday activities.	**A Holder of Values:** ■ has a set of clearly defined personal values. ■ "walks the talk" of personal core values. ■ encourages others to develop, define and live personal values. ■ understands the organization's values and uses them as a foundational purpose for all efforts. ■ understands and encourages the consistent use of organizational guiding principles that are observable, measurable, and replicable by others. ■ protects their personal and organizational values from becoming eroded. ■ models authenticity; personal and professional life is seamless. ■ encourages values-driven achievement in others.

**Every accomplishment,
every achievement,
every success
begins with vision.**

LEGACY LEADERSHIP® INSTITUTE PARTICIPANT WORKBOOK © 2001-2016. COACHWORKS® International. Dallas, TX USA. All Rights Reserved.
Page 165

Legacy Steps

1

Holding **VISION**	*Holding* **VALUES**
1. Determine the organization's vision statement(s). If necessary, this may need to be re-stated, re-worked, re-affirmed, or whatever is necessary to provide a clear tool and written communication of organization's vision.	1. Determine the organization's values statement(s). If necessary, this may need to be re-stated, re-worked, re-affirmed, or whatever is necessary to provide a clear tool and written communication of organization's values. How does this company want to be known in the workplace? What values are important? Once values are defined and clearly identified—KNOW them!
2. Determine how (lay out a plan) you will explain, communicate this easily to clients, other employees.	2. Openly and frequently communicate the values to all employees at every level, encouraging their buy-in and cooperation.
3. Openly and frequently communicate the vision to all employees at every level, encouraging their buy-in and cooperation.	3. Assure that every decision or action is held up to organizational values. Discard those that do not match up. No compromise.
4. Assure that every decision or action is held up to the organizational vision. Discard those that do not match up.	4. Be sure organizational values are reflected in every activity so that it becomes an automatic "reflex."
5. Be sure organizational vision is kept as foundation of every project and goal until it becomes an automatic "reflex."	5. Be able to easily articulate the organizational (as well as your personal) values for both clients and fellow team members. The talk is important, but remember that the walk is the loudest communicator.
6. Be able to easily articulate the organizational (as well as your personal) vision for both clients and fellow team members.	6. Alert team members when particular values may be compromised during any decision making process.
7. Formulate personal vision in written and measurable format, and internalize for use in achievement of organizational vision.	7. Avoid self righteousness!
8. Bring whole self to your leadership.	8. The organization's reputation is your reputation. Consider this when representing your organization to the public or fellow team members.
9. Understand that what you do and say today shapes the future.	9. Determine how you might uphold your personal core values when and if you find that they do not match your organization's values.
10. Make organizational vision compelling, inspiring to others.	10. Do not attempt to "cover up" mistakes, or the compromising of values.

Language

1	*Holding* **VISION**	*Holding* **VALUES**
Statements	■ Language that matches vision to process. ■ Language that matches and reminds of vision. ■ Language that praises and commends matching of vision to process.	■ Language that insures process, decision and action matches values. ■ Language that upholds values. ■ Language that allows for course correction to values.
Questions	■ Questions that remind and assure understanding of vision. ■ Questions that remind all to measure against vision. ■ Questions that assure all can articulate and incorporate vision.	■ Questions that remind and assure understanding of values. ■ Questions that remind all to measure against values (personal and organizational). ■ Questions that assure all can articulate and incorporate values.

1

	Holding **VISION**	Holding **VALUES**
(the Legacy Leader® CREATES the environment that generates these shifts)	■ **FROM fuzzy...TO focused** Instead of a team working with fuzzy, uncommunicated, and poorly stated vision and goals, each individual is empowered with a clear understanding of organizational vision, allowing them to work in a focused and targeted manner. ■ **FROM "wandering lost..." TO following roadmaps and milestones** Instead of employees wandering through their activities with no apparent strategy, hoping to meet unstated goals, individuals are given clear roadmaps and stated milestones along the way, with consistent guidance in "map-reading" skills. ■ **FROM no personal direction...TO well-defined personal vision and goals** Employees who previously had no personal vision are encouraged to define their own goals and use them to drive their personal and corporate contribution to meeting the organizational vision.	■ **FROM lack of operational policies... TO well communicated guiding principles** Instead of individuals performing in random and occasionally "out of bounds" methods, all behavior is guided by consistent and well communicated values. ■ **FROM bad or no reputation... TO reputation for excellence** Instead of an organization about which only unfavorable or missing reputation is available (inside or outside the organization), the organization begins to be a "name brand" based on reputation for excellence in all phases of operation and performance. A Legacy Leadership® company's branding is noteworthy and respected. ■ **FROM "cover-ups"...TO open pride** Instead of constantly "covering up" behavior or performance that is below the level of acceptable business ethics and values, individuals, teams and leadership begin to take pride and ownership in an organization that holds values as priorities, in consistent and illuminating ways. This behavior spreads from the organizational level to every employee.

"First say to yourself what you
would be; and then do
what you have
to do."
—*Epictetus*

1

Holder of Vision and Values™

In order to enhance the practical application of Legacy Leadership®, each of the 5 Best Practices contains 10 Critical Success Skills. These skills contain the competencies, attitudes and behaviors which are the hallmark of great leaders. These 10 skills/ competencies are the basis of the ten assessment questions for Best Practice 1 in the Legacy Leadership® Competency Inventory (LLCI)™.

CRITICAL SUCCESS SKILLS

1. Consistently reinforce the organization's vision and values.

2. Intentionally model guiding principles in everything, with everyone.

3. Personally integrate organization's vision in all responsibilities.

4. Have well-defined strategic plan for accomplishing vision.

5. Enable team to translate organizational vision, and align daily responsibilities with organizational goals.

6. Establish measurable milestones congruent with vision.

7. Ensure that organizational values are integrated into how organization does business.

8. Clearly identify personal values; "walk the talk" in everything.

9. Place importance on developing others.

10. Effectively communicate, sustain processes to achieve vision and values.

1

Holder of Vision and Values™

A HOLDER "keeps in hand" those things that are important, embracing and encouraging their remembrance.

Definition	**VISION** is a clear view and understanding of realizable goals, plans and intentions.	**VALUES** are those things considered right, worthwhile, and desirable—the basis of guiding principles and standards.
What it IS: The Legacy Leader® will:	▪ hold vision by being clear on both personal and organizational vision and by measuring all ideas, decisions, commitment and actions against the organization's vision template. ▪ encourage, promote and protect such organizational vision by embracing and encouraging its remembrance. ▪ establish and maintain this vision "holding" so that it becomes foundational to all activities.	▪ hold values by being clear on both personal and organizational guiding principles and standards and by measuring all ideas, decisions, commitment and actions against the organization's values template. ▪ encourage, promote and protect these values by embracing them, modeling them and encouraging their remembrance. ▪ establish and maintain this values "holding" so that it becomes foundational to all activities.
What it is NOT:	▪ Vague reference to non-measurable goals ▪ A ruler to "slap hands" ▪ Harboring "secret information"	▪ Enforcing "rules" ▪ Merely acknowledging a behavior code ▪ Self righteousness
Factors for Success (what must be in place)	▪ Clear compelling organizational vision in writing ▪ Excellent communication of vision throughout organization ▪ Ways to measure vision ▪ Roadmap and milestones ▪ Compelling strategic design throughout organization ▪ Knowledge of personal vision/match to organizational vision	▪ Fully developed values statement and guiding principles that are clearly defined ▪ Organization-wide communication of values ▪ Measurement methods ▪ Employee clarity and acceptance of values ▪ Attitude of values underlying all work
Challenges (Potential Barriers)	▪ No existing written or communicated organizational vision ▪ Teammates are not invested or interested in organizational vision — are self interested ▪ Existing vision is not compelling, inspiring ▪ Existing vision is not measurable	▪ No established organizational values, guiding principles ▪ Leadership does not model values ▪ Individual "renegades" as exception to expected behavior ▪ Existing values not "owned" by employees ▪ Individuals with conflicting personal values
Behaviors and Competencies **The Holder of this will...**	▪ have a well-defined personal vision. ▪ clearly understand organization's vision and use it as a foundational purpose for all efforts. ▪ have clear alignment with organization's vision, and its relationship with all individuals, teams, and activities. ▪ bring his or her whole self to this leadership model. ▪ consistently communicate and strategize around, and measure performance against organizational vision. ▪ encourage others to create their own vision. ▪ protect the vision from being diminished. ▪ provide consistent focus and direction. ▪ make vision exciting, help it come alive in daily activities.	▪ have a set of clearly defined personal values. ▪ "walk the talk" of personal core values. ▪ encourage others to develop, define and live personal values. ▪ understand the organization's values and use them as a foundational purpose for all efforts. ▪ understand and encourage consistent use of organizational guiding principles that are observable, measurable, and replicable by others. ▪ protect personal and organizational values from becoming eroded. ▪ model authenticity. Personal, professional life seamless. ▪ encourage values-driven achievement in others.
***LegacyShifts*™**	▪ FROM fuzzy TO focused ▪ FROM "wandering lost" TO following roadmaps, milestones ▪ FROM no personal direction TO well-defined personal vision, goals	▪ FROM lack of operational policies TO well communicated guiding principles ▪ FROM bad or no reputation TO reputation for excellence ▪ FROM "cover-ups" TO open pride
Legacy Steps	▪ Determine organization's vision statement(s). Re-state, re-work, re-affirm as necessary for clear communication. ▪ Plan how you will explain, communicate this easily. ▪ Openly, frequently communicate vision at every level, encouraging buy-in and cooperation. ▪ Hold up every decision/action to organizational vision. Discard those that do not match up. ▪ Be sure vision is kept as foundation of every project and goal until it becomes an automatic "reflex." ▪ Be able to easily articulate the organizational (as well as personal) vision for both. ▪ Formulate personal vision in written and measurable format, internalize for use in achievement of organizational vision. ▪ Bring whole self to your leadership. ▪ Understand that what you do and say today shapes the future. ▪ 10. Make organizational vision compelling, inspiring to others.	▪ Determine organization's values statement(s). How does this company want to be known in the workplace? ▪ Openly, frequently communicate values at every level, encouraging buy-in, cooperation. ▪ Hold up every decision or action to organizational values. Discard non-matches. No compromise. ▪ Be sure organizational values are reflected in every activity so that it becomes automatic "reflex." ▪ Be able to easily articulate organizational/personal values—talk is important, but walk is loudest. ▪ Alert team members when values may be compromised. ▪ Avoid self righteousness! ▪ Remember, organization's reputation is your reputation. ▪ Determine how you will uphold personal core values when and if they do not match organization's values. ▪ 10. Don't "cover up" mistakes, compromise values.

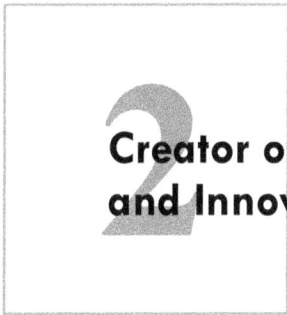

2 Creator of Collaboration and Innovation™

2 Creator of Collaboration and Innovation™

Basic Definitions

Creator

A CREATOR causes something to "come into being" often through original or inventive means.

Collaboration

COLLABORATION is the process of working together to achieve common goals instead of personal agenda.

Innovation

INNOVATION is the introduction of something new and different to the process of achieving goals.

Legacy Leadership® Definitions

The Legacy Leader® will create collaboration and innovation by:

- gathering people with differing perspectives, talents, gifts, and attitudes for the purpose of creating something bigger, better and more significant than any one of them could have done alone.

- challenging current thinking and assumptions, encouraging the creation and installation of better ways and ideas, and by role-modeling for the team or community imaginative and inventive visualization beyond the present reality. Innovation is the product of creative collaboration

- encouraging, promoting and protecting collaborative innovation through a variety of inventive means.

- establishing and maintaining this collaborative innovation so that it becomes foundational to all activities.

2

Creating **COLLABORATION**	*Creating* **INNOVATION**
Creating Collaboration is NOT: ■ **Forced cooperation** Collaboration created by a Legacy Leader® is NOT the mandate of forced cooperation. Cooperation implies being on separate pages and coming together out of necessity. Created collaboration IS the page. ■ **Impromptu Brainstorming** Collaboration created by Legacy Leadership® is NOT the spontaneous or impromptu brainstorming session, which is freeform, open-ended and completely unstructured. Created collaboration is collective, structured, nurtured and is an attitude that is foundational to all activities. ■ **Fostered Competition** Collaboration created by Legacy Leadership® is NOT the fostering of individual competition or self-protection within a "group" to see who can best the other. Created collaboration is the genuine mutual interest in one another, and particularly in the shared project or organizational goals.	**Creating Innovation is NOT:** ■ **Visioning and Futuristic Thinking** Innovation created by a Legacy Leader® is NOT the dictation of future thinking. Visioning, or seeing a "future" place or state, is about thinking of the future. Innovation is about thinking and doing in creative ways to get to the future. ■ **Creativity** Innovation created by Legacy Leadership® is NOT the individual use of a gift or talent. Created innovation is the collaborative product of combined creative processes from a stimulated and nurtured community. ■ **Change for Change Sake** Innovation created by Legacy Leadership® is NOT the institution of change merely for the sake of change. Created innovation may lead to change, but that change will bring a universally better product, service or process.

Critical Factors

2	*Creating* **COLLABORATION**	*Creating* **INNOVATION**
Factors for Success	• High levels of trust throughout organization • A "team" mindset to achieve common goals • Processes for building collaboration • Processes for capturing outcomes • Everyone assumes personal responsibility for bringing their best to the table • Established process for follow-through	• A creative environment • A commitment to innovation and innovative thinking • High levels of trust • Framework for collaboration • "No boundaries" in thought processes
Challenges (Potential Barriers)	• No existing process for collaboration (an environment that does not allow for free exchange of ideas) • Teammates are self-interested, not community-interested • Employee disrespect for fellow workers • Lack of trust • Lack of collaborative skills or mindset • Resistance to creating something new (stuck in comfort zone)	• Fear of change ("Things are just fine the way they are...") • Focus on past or present • Fear of real success • Dissenters/Narrow thinkers ("We can't do that." "That won't work.")

Application

2	*Creating* **COLLABORATION**	*Creating* **INNOVATION**
Behaviors and Competencies	**A Creator of Collaboration:** ▪ looks for ways to create a collaborative circle among existing teams, structures, etc. ▪ is inventive in this endeavor, encouraging communication and openness. ▪ puts aside ego to hear the brilliance of others. ▪ is specific about shared goals and interests. ▪ brings out the best in others. ▪ asks the tough questions (ones he or she does not know the answers to), and hears the answers. ▪ creates an atmosphere of flexibility and adaptability ▪ works to put aside fears of creative tension.	**A Creator of Innovation:** ▪ does a variety of things to enhance his or her own personal creativity. ▪ looks for areas where mistrust may be a hurdle, and works to remove it. ▪ opens closed "boxes" for others to see inside and outside. ▪ generates excitement for shared innovation and results. ▪ challenges thinking "outside the norm." ▪ has the ability to shift quickly — personal "agility." ▪ embraces change as great opportunity. ▪ encourages continual learning.

Legacy Steps

2

Creating COLLABORATION	Creating INNOVATION
1. Be respectful. Showing respect builds trust.	1. Clearly identify the challenge(s).
2. Listen thoroughly. Know what you're talking about before you talk.	2. Gather together a group of cross-functional individuals with unique perspectives and responsibilities.
3. Honor differences of opinion. Understand how differences can build information.	3. Clearly establish the process in which you are about to engage. Reaffirm value of everyone's input.
4. Create atmosphere where everyone can be heard and feel free to contribute.	4. Set the ground rules. (i.e., no discussion about negative behavior or how "we got into this situation" – no past blaming, only future creating, all ideas worth exploring, think outside box, etc.)
4. Encourage everyone's participation. No holdouts!	
5. Communicate expectations of collaboration (what does it look like?).	5. Set up question: "What do we have to change to have this (goal, vision, etc.) happen?
6. Acknowledge equal ranking to all ideas. Set judgment aside. Be open minded.	6. Set parameters, boundaries, etc.
7. Focus on "greater good" of organization, beyond the team framework. (Keep vision and values in sight.)	7. Openly work collaboratively to design process, communication connections, to achieve stated goal.
	8. Do not judge ideas until all innovative thinking is on the table.
8. Become familiar with strengths of teammates, perspectives, gifts, points of view, etc.	9. All ideas are in writing and all process evaluation is documented, logged for review.
9. Make interaction fun and invigorating.	10. Share all ideas, share all processing, share all input/feedback, share in final product.
10. Speak the truth with respect and clarity.	

Language

2	*Creating* **COLLABORATION**	*Creating* **INNOVATION**
Statements	<ul><li>Language that explains back.</li><li>Language that elaborates, understands the first idea, then adds to it.</li><li>Language that affirms the individual.</li><li>Language that sets the tone for collaboration.</li></ul>	<ul><li>Statements that open doors to new thinking.</li><li>Statements that disregard past things or methods and encourage individuals to go beyond.</li><li>Statements to call for stretching and creativity as a unit.</li></ul>
Questions	<ul><li>Questions that seek to know the individual.</li><li>Questions that assure all understand the process.</li><li>Questions that seek combined potential and success.</li></ul>	<ul><li>Questions that compare reality to where you want to be.</li><li>Questions that seek answers for making reality and future goals match.</li><li>Questions that turn limitations and boundaries into limitless opportunity.</li></ul>

2	*Creating* **COLLABORATION**	*Creating* **INNOVATION**
(the Legacy Leader® CREATES the environment that generates these shifts)	■ **FROM judgment...** **TO curiosity** Instead of judging fellow workers, employees begin wondering what they could collaboratively accomplish. ■ **FROM "ho hum" meetings...** **TO "ah hah!" sessions** Instead of non-productive business as usual meetings, employees anticipate group sessions with expectation for discovery and accomplishment. ■ **FROM suspicion...** **TO trust** Getting to know one another and working collaboratively erases suspicion, the need to protect self and competition, and fosters an environment of trust, critical to collaboration.	■ **FROM ordinary...** **TO extraordinary** Instead of ordinary thinking, team members learn to automatically think beyond to the extraordinary, the unusual, the innovative. ■ **FROM focus on past...** **TO focus on future** Instead of focusing on what has already been, or is being accomplished, a new excitement for the future potential becomes part of innovative thinking. ■ **FROM fear of change...** **TO embracing the new** Instead of fearing change, a human response, employees learn from the behavior of the Legacy Leader®, that change holds huge potential for exciting new ways to meet goals.

Leaders must admit they don't know everything, and don't have all the answers.

Critical Success Skills

2 Creator of Collaboration and Innovation™

In order to enhance the practical application of Legacy Leadership®, each of the 5 Best Practices contains 10 Critical Success Skills. These skills contain the competencies, attitudes and behaviors which are the hallmark of great leaders. These 10 skills/competencies are the basis of the ten assessment questions for Best Practice 2 in the Legacy Leadership® Competency Inventory (LLCI)™.

CRITICAL SUCCESS SKILLS

1. Create innovative and sound possibilities for the organization.

2. Foster learning, trusting environment for true collaboration and innovation.

3. Masterfully listen for both what is said and what is not said.

4. Be comfortable not knowing "the answers" and learn from individual perspectives.

5. Draw out differing perspectives and believe disagreement is a learning opportunity.

6. Ask timely, tough questions while keeping in mind the big picture.

7. Set the tone for thinking beyond the present for innovative future.

8. Project how ideas will play out in the organization and marketplace.

9. Discern, and assist others to understand, when change needs to happen and when it does not.

10. Masterfully facilitate conversations where everyone contributes best thinking toward task/goal.

Creator of Collaboration and Innovation™

A CREATOR causes something to "come into being" often through original or inventive means.

	COLLABORATION	INNOVATION
Definition	COLLABORATION is the process of working together to achieve common goals instead of personal agenda.	INNOVATION is the introduction of something new and different to the process of achieving goals.
What it IS: The Legacy Leader® will:	▪ create collaboration by gathering people with differing perspectives, talents, gifts, and attitudes for the purpose of creating something bigger, better and more significant than any one of them could have done alone. ▪ encourage, promote and protect such collaboration through a variety of inventive means. ▪ establish and maintain this collaborative process so that it becomes foundational to all activities.	▪ create innovation by challenging current thinking and assumptions, encouraging the creation and installation of better ways and ideas, and by role-modeling for the team or community imaginative and inventive visualization beyond the present reality. Innovation is the product of creative collaboration. ▪ encourage, promote and protect such collaborative innovation through a variety of inventive means. ▪ maintain this innovative process so that it becomes foundational to all activities.
What it is NOT:	▪ Forced cooperation ▪ Impromptu Brainstorming ▪ Fostered Competition	▪ Visioning and Futuristic Thinking ▪ Creativity ▪ Change for Change Sake
Factors for Success (what must be in place)	▪ High levels of trust ▪ A "team" mindset ▪ Processes for building collaboration, capturing outcomes, follow through ▪ Personal responsibility	▪ A creative environment ▪ A commitment to innovation ▪ High levels of trust ▪ Framework for collaboration ▪ "No boundaries" in thought processes
Challenges (Potential Barriers)	▪ No process for collaboration (environment that does not allow for free exchange of ideas) ▪ Teammates self-interested, not community interested ▪ Employee disrespect ▪ Lack of trust ▪ Lack of collaborative skills or mindset ▪ Resistance to creating something new (stuck in comfort zone)	▪ Fear of change ▪ Focus on past or present ▪ Fear of real success ▪ Dissenters/Narrow thinkers ("We can't do that." "That won't work.")
Behaviors and Competencies **The Holder of this will...**	▪ look for ways to create a collaborative circle among existing teams, structures, etc. ▪ be inventive, encouraging communication and openness. ▪ put aside ego to hear the brilliance of others. ▪ be specific about shared goals and interests. ▪ bring out the best in others. ▪ ask the tough questions and hear the answers. ▪ create an atmosphere of flexibility and adaptability ▪ put aside fears of creative tension.	▪ do a variety of things to enhance their own personal creativity. ▪ look for areas where mistrust may be a hurdle, and work to remove it. ▪ open closed "boxes" for others to see inside and outside. ▪ generate excitement for shared innovation and results. ▪ challenge thinking "outside the norm." ▪ have the ability to shift quickly — personal "agility." ▪ embrace change as great opportunity. ▪ encourage continual learning.
LegacyShifts™	▪ FROM judgment TO curiosity ▪ FROM "ho hum" meetings TO "ah hah!" sessions ▪ FROM suspicion TO trust	▪ FROM ordinary TO extraordinary ▪ FROM focus on past TO focus on future ▪ FROM fear of change TO embracing the new
Legacy Steps	1. Be respectful. 2. Listen thoroughly. 3. Honor differences of opinion. 4. Create atmosphere where everyone is heard, feels free to contribute. 5. Encourage everyone's participation. 6. Communicate expectations of collaboration. 7. Give equal ranking to all ideas. Set judgment aside. Be open minded. 8. Focus on "greater good" of organization. 9. Become familiar with strengths of teammates, perspectives, gifts, points of view, etc. 10. Make interaction fun, invigorating. 11. Speak the truth with respect and clarity.	1. Clearly identify challenge(s). 2. Gather together a group of cross-functional individuals with unique perspectives and responsibilities. 3. Clearly establish the process. 4. Set the ground rules, parameters, boundaries, etc. 5. Openly work collaboratively to design process. 6. Do not judge ideas until all innovative thinking is on the table. 7. All ideas in writing and all process documented, logged for review. 8. Share everything.

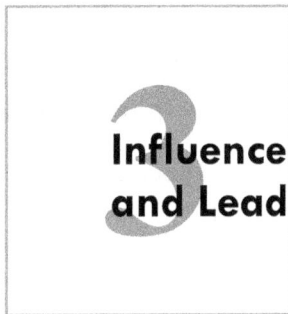

3 Influencer of Inspiration and Leadership™

3

Influencer of Inspiration and Leadership™

Basic Definitions

Influencer

An INFLUENCER brings about a desired effect in others, either by direct or indirect means.

Inspiration

INSPIRATION is the process of animating, motivating or encouraging others to reach new levels of achievement.

Leadership

LEADERSHIP is the process of guiding and directing others to shared success.

Legacy Leadership® Definitions

The Legacy Leader® will influence inspiration and leadership by:

- creating an environment that brings people to life and fills others with energy. In doing so, others will then bring inspiration and life to the organization.

- leading through positive rather than negative influence, AND by encouraging discovery and development of positive leadership styles in others. We believe everyone is a leader, and as such, should have positive influential leaders as role models, and should be encouraged in their own leadership style development.

- growing, promoting and protecting such inspirational leadership by always providing a consistent and positive role model, encouraging ongoing and lasting positive energy and passion in others, and by creating opportunities for learning and discovery of personal leadership styles.

- establishing and maintaining these processes so that they become foundational to all activities.

In order to be inspirational, you have to be inspired yourself.

Inspiration fuels persistence, and promotes discovery.

3

Influencing **INSPIRATION**	*Influencing* **LEADERSHIP**

Influencing Inspiration is NOT:	**Influencing Leadership is NOT:**
■ **Simply Motivation** Inspiration influenced by a Legacy Leader® is NOT simply motivation. A leader cannot motivate someone else, but can inspire someone to motivate themselves. Some forms of motivation may involve fear or discipline, which does not elicit the best from others. ■ **"Pumping Up"** Inspiration influenced by Legacy Leadership® is NOT short term pumping up of another in order to evoke some sort of specific response. Pumping up others may provide a short term burst of energy, but is generally not sustained. ■ **Putting on a "Happy Face"** Inspiration influenced by a Legacy Leader® is NOT pasting a "smiling face" over a scowl before you face others. People can discern the difference between genuine inspiration and generated attitude. Legacy Leadership® inspiration is connecting with others personally and deeply, revealing their strengths, using anecdotal stories that genuinely inspire, and understanding what does and does not inspire others. Legacy Leadership® inspiration empowers others to become self-inspired.	■ **"Cloning" Leaders** Leadership influenced by a Legacy Leader® is NOT the cloning or duplication of your own leadership style in others. It is NOT making another YOU. This kind of influence actively seeks to allow discovery and continuous learning and development of individual styles of leadership in the people you lead. ■ **Political Correctness** Leadership influenced by Legacy Leadership® is NOT the attempt to be politically or socially "correct" by speaking a certain language, or acting with certain acceptable behavior. It is the conscious mindset that makes every challenge an opportunity and continually influences through honest and genuinely positive means. ■ **Kingdom or Empire Building** Leadership influenced by a Legacy Leader® does NOT seek to build self-serving empires or "kingdoms" within the organization or corporate landscape, and does NOT create a group of "yes" men and women. Rather, this leadership influence builds individual leaders with positive attitudes and distinctly different styles.

Critical Factors

3	Influencing INSPIRATION	Influencing LEADERSHIP
Factors for Success	■ Strong sense of vision and values ■ Desire to encourage and inspire others ■ Understanding of others' strengths ■ Mental "library" of stories that inspire ■ Understanding of what inspires self, and others ■ Desire and ability to live a role model for others ■ Understanding of own personal passion	■ Ability to influence others in a positive way ■ Ability to look at challenges as opportunities for growth and innovation ■ A desire to be a positive influence on others ■ A solid working knowledge of the cutting edge technology of various leadership models and styles ■ Ability and desire to build relationships ■ Consistent positive thinking ■ Desire to mentor ■ More importance on development of others, rather than self ■ Clear vision and values (personal and organizational)
Challenges (Potential Barriers)	■ Soul-less environment (heart is not included in processes) ■ Teammates are self-interested, not others-interested ■ Employee disrespect for fellow workers ■ Lack of trust ■ Self-protective barriers ■ Organizational rules—separation of business and personal ■ Organizational emphasis on numbers	■ Hidden organizational or personal agendas ■ Lack of knowledge of leadership styles, skills, models ■ Insufficient trust between leader and potential leader ■ Lack of respect for others ■ Organizational command-and-control rather than nurturing structure

Motivation lights a fire.
Inspiration walks a consistent path.

Application

3	*Influencing* **INSPIRATION**	*Influencing* **LEADERSHIP**
Behaviors and Competencies	**An Influencer of Inspiration:** ■ knows him or her self well, and knows what inspires them. ■ is self-inspired, and knows what inspires others. ■ works to discover the strengths of others to better inspire them. ■ expresses a positive, powerful hope for the future - both personally and organizationally. ■ builds trust in others. ■ develops a personal repertoire of inspirational stories. ■ keeps the heart included in all processes. ■ connects personally with others, valuing them individually and corporately. ■ walks a daily path, with even attitude, consistent energy and influential encouragement. ■ has passion and consistency.	**An Influencer of Leadership:** ■ has a positive attitude at all (okay, most!) times. ■ uses positive and uplifting language, even in crisis or other challenging moments. ■ is able to make the right choices in difficult situations. ■ has excellent internal character, principles and values. ■ has an excellent working knowledge of cutting edge leadership technologies, models, styles and language. ■ is a presence for the positive. ■ provides appropriate opportunities to develop the leadership abilities, skills and styles in those they lead. ■ invites rather than commands. ■ actively seeks moments in every day in which to uplift and enhance the growth of others. ■ instills confidence rather than destroying it.

Legacy Steps

3

Influencing **INSPIRATION**	*Influencing* **LEADERSHIP**
1. Develop your ability to successfully influence others to self-motivation and self-inspiration.	1. CHOOSE to be positive.
2. Discover the strengths of others.	2. Open doors, carefully take down walls, and break through any barriers you have built between yourself and others.
3. Learn what inspires others., and develop an attitude of inspiration.	3. Work at your knowledge of various leadership models and styles. Determine what works and what doesn't. Share the news through opportunity. Model what works.
4. Connect personally with others on all levels.	4. Work at building the trust of fellow workers.
5. Develop and tell stories (at appropriate times) that inspire.	5. Get to really know your team members. Understand their strengths, their values, their skills and then actively seek opportunities to encourage them in the use of these gifts to build their own leadership acumen.
6. Challenge and encourage others to work from their strengths.	6. Diffuse conflict and confrontation with positive energy.
7. Focus on living a model of consistent inspiration for others.	7. Thoroughly and honestly evaluate your own leadership intentions and style. Throw out the self-centered and develop the other-centered aspects.
8. Discard old ideas of motivation. Learn and incorporate a new plan for individual and team inspiration.	8. Respect others—always, and regardless!
9. Continue your own process of learning, and being inspired by others.	9. Consider everyone you work with a potential leader— then treat them, model for them, and challenge them as such.
10. Learn how to consistently bring out the best in others.	10. Take care of yourself physically and spiritually! Your well-being in body, mind and spirit will dramatically affect your leadership, and the influence it has over others. Passion and positive energy are directly related to personal well-being, not just professional station.

Language

3	*Influencing* **INSPIRATION**	*Influencing* **LEADERSHIP**
Statements	One of the biggest misconceptions about inspiration is that we can speak a certain "language" and sound inspiring. While telling appropriate inspiring stories is part of influencing inspiration, words alone are not inspirational. There is no real language of inspiration. It is less about what you do and say, and more about who you are, and what you model for others. It is a consistent, real empowering of others through imparted energy and passion.	▪ Statements that promote thinking of possibilities. ▪ Statements that encourage development of leadership potential and strengths in others. ▪ Statements that lead to positive forward thinking instead of dwelling on past and failures, or negative thinking.
Questions	Rather than learn an acceptable "language" of inspiration, we encourage you to develop a repertoire of inspirational stories and anecdotal experiences which can be shared honestly at appropriate moments. Also consider how your actions and attitude are the loudest language you will speak in this Best Practice.	▪ Questions that open doors to personal and organizational growth. ▪ Questions that promote leadership thinking, and the individual's conception of excellent leadership. ▪ Questions that afford opportunities for individuals to be leaders among their peers in given moments.

"There's no greater crime in business today than leaders that de-motivate people. Leadership is about lifting people up and having them do their best."
—*Pat Haggarty,*
CEO of Texas Instruments, 1964

Legacy Shifts ™

3	*Influencing* **INSPIRATION**	*Influencing* **LEADERSHIP**
(the Legacy Leader® CREATES the environment that generates these shifts)	■ **FROM Heartless...** **TO Heartfelt** Instead of heartless day-to-day grind of expected activity, leaders portray a heartfelt interest in others and a desire to inspire. ■ **FROM Pulling Teeth...** **TO Sustained Energy and Passion** Instead of continually working to generate some type of action, response or specific behavior, leaders inspire others to motivate themselves and provide their own inner energy and known passion. ■ **FROM Bringing Down...** **TO Lifting Up** Motivation and discipline can bring people down and either slow, interrupt or completely stop forward progress. True inspiration lifts others up to heights of clarified "air" and environment which advances and speeds progress.	■ **FROM personal power...** **TO empowering others** Instead of claiming the position as "king" or "queen" of the company or department, the Legacy Leader® actively and purposely creates future leaders through consistent modeling of passion and compassion. ■ **FROM a negative attitude...** **TO a BE-attitude** Instead of always seeing the negative, the Legacy Leader® actively changes a "bad" attitude to a CAN BE-attitude and a CAN DO-attitude. Attitude is a choice, regardless of the situation. A Legacy Leader® deliberately chooses the positive. Soon the choice becomes an automatic reflex. ■ **FROM isolationism...** **TO relationalism** Instead of withdrawing into self-protective shells and behind walls or closed doors, the Legacy Leader® deliberately opens doors, establishes relationships and influences others to do the same.

LEGACY LEADERSHIP® INSTITUTE PARTICIPANT WORKBOOK © 2001-2016. COACHWORKS® *International. Dallas, TX USA. All Rights Reserved.*
Page 188

Critical Success Skills

3 Influencer of Inspiration and Leadership™

In order to enhance the practical application of Legacy Leadership®, each of the 5 Best Practices contains 10 Critical Success Skills. These skills contain the competencies, attitudes and behaviors which are the hallmark of great leaders. These 10 skills/competencies are the basis of the ten assessment questions for Best Practice 3 in the Legacy Leadership® Competency Inventory (LLCI)™.

CRITICAL SUCCESS SKILLS

1. Be adept at developing, maintaining relationships.

2. Use emotional intelligence, positive energy to influence others.

3. Choose to model positive perspective in all situations.

4. Bring out the best in people.

5. Constantly acknowledge and recognize attributes and contributions of others.

6. Intentionally delegate for development of others.

7. Lead with constant focus on showcasing others, not self.

8. Have ability and courage to take risks and inspire others to follow.

9. Be able to make tough decisions with minimal negative impact

10. Lead with humility and fierce resolve to accomplish goals through others.

Influencer of Inspiration and Leadership™

An INFLUENCER brings about a desired effect in others, either by direct or indirect means.

	INSPIRATION is the process of animating, motivating or encouraging others to reach new levels of achievement.	LEADERSHIP is the process of guiding and directing others to shared success.
Definition		
What it IS: The Legacy Leader® will:	▪ Influence inspiration by creating an environment that brings people to life and fills others with energy. In doing so, others will then bring inspiration and life to the organization. ▪ encourage, promote and protect such inspiration by encouraging ongoing and lasting positive energy and passion in others by providing a consistent model. ▪ establish and maintain this inspirational process so that it becomes foundational to all activities.	▪ Influence the leadership both OF and IN others by leading through positive rather than negative influence, AND by encouraging the discovery and development of positive leadership styles in others. We believe everyone is a leader, and as such, should have positive influential leaders as role models, and be encouraged in their own leadership style development. ▪ encourage, promote and protect this influential leadership by always providing a positive role model, and by creating opportunities for learning and discovery of personal leadership styles. ▪ maintain this influential leadership process so that it becomes foundational to all activities.
What it is NOT:	▪ Simply motivation ▪ "Pumping Up" ▪ Putting on a "happy face"	▪ "Cloning" leaders ▪ Political correctness ▪ Kingdom or Empire Building
Factors for Success (what must be in place)	▪ Strong sense of vision and values ▪ Desire to encourage and inspire others ▪ Understanding of others' strengths ▪ Mental "library" of stories that inspire ▪ Understanding of what inspires self, and others ▪ Desire and ability to live a role model for others ▪ Understanding of own personal passion	▪ Ability/desire to influence others in a positive way ▪ Ability to look at challenges as opportunities for growth ▪ A solid working knowledge of the cutting edge technology of various leadership models and styles ▪ Ability and desire to build relationships ▪ Consistent positive thinking ▪ Desire to mentor ▪ More importance on development of others, rather than self ▪ Clear vision and values (personal and organizational)
Challenges (Potential Barriers)	▪ Soul-less environment (heart is not included in processes) ▪ Teammates are self-interested, not others-interested ▪ Employee disrespect for fellow workers ▪ Lack of trust ▪ Self-protective barriers ▪ Organizational rules—separation of business and personal ▪ Organizational emphasis on numbers	▪ Hidden organizational or personal agendas ▪ Lack of knowledge of leadership styles, skills, models ▪ Insufficient trust between leader and potential leader ▪ Lack of respect for others ▪ Organizational command-and-control rather than nurturing structure
Behaviors and Competencies **The Holder of this will...**	▪ know him or her self well, and what inspires them. ▪ be self-inspired, and know what inspires others. ▪ work to discover the strengths of others to better inspire them. ▪ express a positive, powerful hope for the future - both personally and organizationally. ▪ build trust in others. ▪ develop a personal repertoire of inspirational stories. ▪ keep the heart included in all processes. ▪ connect personally/others, value individually and corporately. ▪ walk a daily path, with even attitude, consistent energy and influential encouragement. ▪ have passion and consistency.	▪ have a positive attitude at all (okay, most!) times. ▪ use positive and uplifting language, even in crisis or other challenging moments. ▪ be able to make the right choices in difficult situations. ▪ have excellent internal character, principles and values. ▪ have an excellent working knowledge of cutting edge leadership technologies, model, styles and language. ▪ provide appropriate opportunities to develop the leadership abilities, skills and styles in those they lead. ▪ invite rather than commands. ▪ seek moments each day to uplift, enhance growth of others. ▪ instill confidence rather than destroying it.
LegacyShifts™	▪ FROM heartless TO heartfelt ▪ FROM pulling teeth TO sustained energy and passion ▪ FROM bringing down TO lifting up	▪ FROM personal power TO empowering others ▪ FROM a negative attitude TO a BE-attitude ▪ FROM isolationism TO relationalism
Legacy Steps	1. Develop ability to successfully influence others to self-motivation, self-inspiration. 2. Discover strengths of others. 3. Learn what inspires others. 4. Develop an attitude of inspiration. 4. Connect personally with others on all levels. 5. Develop and tell stories (at appropriate times) that inspire. 6. Challenge and encourage others to work from their strengths. 7. Focus on living a model of consistent inspiration for others. 8. Discard old ideas of motivation. 9. Continue personal learning, and being inspired by others. 10. Learn how to consistently bring out the best in others.	1. CHOOSE to be positive. 2. Open doors, take down walls, and break through any barriers between yourself and others. 3. Build knowledge of various leadership models and styles. Determine what works and what doesn't. Model what works. 4. Work at building the trust of fellow workers. 5. Get to really know your team members. 6. Diffuse conflict and confrontation with positive energy. 7. Honestly evaluate own leadership intentions/style. Throw out self-centered, develop other-centered aspects. 8. Respect others—always, and regardless! 9. Consider everyone you work with a potential leader. 10. Take care of yourself physically and spiritually!

4

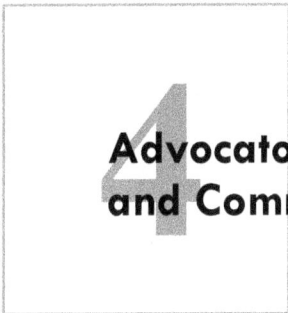

Advocator of Differences and Community™

4 Advocator of Differences and Community™

Basic Definitions

Advocator

An ADVOCATOR stands in support of a cause, a practice or a person on its or their behalf.

Differences

DIFFERENCES are those qualities that distinguish people or things from other people or things.

Community

COMMUNITY is a group of people with shared interest working together to achieve shared success.

Legacy Leadership® Definitions

The Legacy Leader® will advocate differences and community by:

- seeking relationships with team members, by discovering, acknowledging, and accepting differences in those relationships, and by promoting individual strengths and perspectives for the greater whole of the organization.

- promoting and combining differences into a unified whole, and then standing in support of this community as it builds relationships – from within and without the organization – that enlarge and expand the growth of the community and the success of the organization.

- by helping individuals and teams discover strengths in both commonality and differences that can be instrumental in the growth of the individual, the community and the organization, and by modeling an attitude of connectedness and inclusion.

- encouraging, promoting and protecting such advocacy and drawing together individuals who contribute diverse perspectives for a greater good, and who will model the endorsement and leveraging of differences into added value for the whole.

- establishing and maintaining this advocacy so that it becomes foundational to all activities.

> Every relationship on the face of this planet consists of members with differences—large and small—from families to mega-mergers. Unless these differences are accepted, supported and even exalted, none of these relationships will survive.

4

Advocating **DIFFERENCES**	*Advocating* **COMMUNITY**
Advocating Differences is NOT:	**Advocating Community is NOT:**
■ **Equal Employment Opportunity** Differences advocated by a Legacy Leader® are NOT just the practice of EEO. These differences are not necessarily about external appearance, gender, age, orientation or faith. Every person has a unique style, a different perspective, diverse experiences—we are all "wired" differently. Advocating of differences is actively being inclusive of all these varied "unique-nesses" in individuals.	■ **Manipulation** Community advocated by a Legacy Leader® is NOT the manipulation of and "playing up" to others to advance self or "departmentalized" goals and agendas. The advocacy of community by a Legacy Leader is an honest belief and attitude that the organization is a relational community comprised of valued sameness and differences, all of which contribute to the strength of the whole.
■ **The token "oddball"** The advocating of differences by Legacy Leadership® is NOT including the token outsider or oddball into the inner circle, for the sake of appearances. Legacy leadership advocates the inclusion of ALL diversities for a community of perspectives to strengthen the whole.	■ **"Rally 'round the flag" time** The advocating of community through Legacy Leadership® is NOT a spontaneous effort to rally the troops for battle against a common enemy— usually the bottom line of a corporate P&L. It is a persistent and consistent attitude that this organization is whole only because of its many varied and valued parts, and a clear modeling of support and advocacy for the role and contribution of each part to the whole.
■ **Giving "lip service"** The Legacy Leader does NOT give mere "lip service" to differences. The Legacy Leadership® style of advocating differences means to actively and whole-heartedly gather differences into harmonious relationship to promote the "esprit de corps" and the overall well-being of the organization these individuals represent and serve.	■ **Forced inclusion** A community advocated by a Legacy Leader® is NOT enforced or commanded inclusion of "outsiders," but a heartfelt desire for the good of the whole because of contributions of each member. It is an open invitation to use individual differences and perspectives to achieve shared success.

Critical Factors

4	*Advocating* **DIFFERENCES**	*Advocating* **COMMUNITY**
Factors for Success	■ Acknowledgement of the importance and benefit of differences ■ Environment that promotes relationships ■ Openness to diverse perspectives ■ Complete lack of prejudices or other difference-limiting mindsets ■ Passion for learning, discovery ■ Individual egos that take a backseat to wholeness ■ Lack of labels and stereotypes	■ Good team-building environment ■ Acknowledgement that all parts are needed to make the whole ■ Management that promotes community ■ Understanding of the strength afforded in differences ■ Keen desire to know others as people, not pawns ■ Understanding that as one grows and succeeds, ALL do ■ Ability to unite differences into community process ■ Desire to embrace/incorporate diversity in all activities ■ Excellent, consistent, and clear communication
Challenges (Potential Barriers)	■ Labels and prejudices ■ Turf protection ("them" against "us") ■ Comfort zones ■ "Rubber stamp" or "cookie cutter" mentality ■ Non-inclusive belief systems ■ "First sight" snap judgments ■ Inability to see beyond appearances	■ Hidden, or even stated, organizational or personal agendas ■ Organizational or personal lack of concern for others ■ A need to get the "credit" for successes ■ Lack of respect for others ■ Organizational command-and-control rather than relational environment ■ Inability to see the "trees" for the forest ■ Personal, departmental or organizational "walls" or other divisions and separators ■ Communication deficiencies

4	*Advocating* **DIFFERENCES**	*Advocating* **COMMUNITY**
Behaviors and Competencies	**An Advocator of Differences:** ■ actively promotes differences and values them for the organizational whole. ■ acknowledges their own set of biases, stereotypes and labels, then seeks to overcome them. ■ knows how he or she is different. ■ seeks to discover how others see the world and individual situations. ■ is curious about differences, and truly desires to learn more about them. ■ reframes how they think and how they approach people who are "different" from themselves. ■ practices active and interested listening. ■ recaps and summarizes conversation so everyone is clear about content, focus and direction. ■ actively seeks common ground and common good in an environment of differences. ■ takes the time and has the courage to go outside their comfort zone with others. ■ practices being comfortable around those who previously evoked "discomfort."	**An Advocator of Community:** ■ is always looking for the strengths of individuals to add to the success of the whole. ■ sees beyond the boundaries of individuals, teams or departments. ■ always has the success of the whole organization in mind. ■ is knowledgeable about the perspectives, strengths and offerings available from all sources. ■ actively seeks to lift up others, even those "outside" immediate corporate or departmental lines. ■ is aware of the added benefits of inclusion. ■ helps others discover and value their strengths and potential contributions. ■ has identified his or her own strengths. ■ communicates well and often with all possible and necessary parts of the whole. ■ defends, supports and speaks up for their community.

Legacy Steps

4 *Advocating* **DIFFERENCES**	*Advocating* **COMMUNITY**
1. Set aside your ego.	1. CHOOSE to be inclusive.
2. Discover and actively work to overcome your personal biases, prejudices and stereotypes.	2. Open doors, carefully take down walls, and break through any barriers you have built between yourself and others.
3. Actively seek out differences and the strengths within them.	3. Seek every opportunity to acknowledge and respect the contributions of others.
4. Look for common ground where you previously saw only islands of difference.	4. Help others discover their strengths, and potential contribution to the whole.
5. Reframe how you think and approach people that are "different." Take time and make the effort to understand others.	5. Evaluate your existing communication protocols and habits, then work to widen the circle and increase the frequency and informative content.
6. Become an active and eager listener.	6. Practice sharing information with those outside your perceived departmental or team boundaries.
7. Actively seek out the opinions of those who may think differently, and value them.	7. Discover your own unique strengths and perspectives.
8. Design conversations and meetings to be inclusive, then recap for understanding.	8. Remind yourself that you are serving the vision of the whole organization, and that involves every individual, every team, and every department.
9. Remember that you don't have all the answers and other perspectives can provide valuable insight.	9. Support and defend the community as a whole, and bring to light activities or behaviors that do not have this effect.
10. Discard old ideas of territorialism and self-protection, work to lift up others, and understand that many parts make a whole.	10. Be a leader who enables rather than hobbles the growth and inclusion of all people within the whole organizational community.

Language

4	*Advocating* **DIFFERENCES**	*Advocating* **COMMUNITY**
Statements	▪ Statements that give value to the worth of all contributors, and all contributions, and encourage a voice for all. ▪ Statements that acknowledge that I don't have all the answers here. I need everyone's input to make the right choices for our direction. ▪ Statements that appreciate contributions and value of all contributors.	▪ Statements that are inclusive, inviting community participation. ▪ Statements that acknowledge limited understanding without the whole community's input. ▪ Statements that celebrate the unique backgrounds and insights of others, and how that contributes to the whole.
Questions	▪ Questions that open doors to the contributions of other departments, other people, other ways of thinking. ▪ Questions that hold all accountable to being an advocate for the existence and value of differences. ▪ Questions that encourage and invite all to share their own impressions and perspectives in order to get a complete picture.	▪ Questions that facilitate others to use all resources at hand, including other people, departments, etc. ▪ Questions that remind about and encourage "community" communication. ▪ Questions that elicit thinking about the effect of actions, plans, and thoughts on others outside the immediate "circle," team, or department.

Consider this:
Are your words and actions
UNIFYING or DIVIDING?

Are you considering the
WHOLE?

Legacy Shifts ™

4	*Advocating* **DIFFERENCES**	*Advocating* **COMMUNITY**
(the Legacy Leader® CREATES the environment that generates these shifts)	■ **FROM "us against them..."** **TO esprit de corps** Instead of inter-departmental/ positional and territorial posturing and exclusion, an attitude of "we're all in this together" is promoted and celebrated. Every position, every department, every person is acknowledged and encouraged for their valuable contribution to the whole. ■ **FROM "he doesn't have a clue..."** **TO "what can he share?"** Instead of snap labels, personal prejudices and excluding biases that shut down communication and contribution, an actively encouraged attitude of inclusion opens doors to new perspectives, unique possibilities, and greater potential. ■ **FROM Individuals...** **TO Relationships** Individuals working individually cannot accomplish nearly what individuals working in relationship can achieve. When an attitude of openly accepting differences is promoted, a unique connectivity is the result, one which energizes and advances both the individual and the relationship—and the organizational vision.	■ **FROM exclusion...** **TO inclusion** Instead of excluding the thoughts, ideas, strengths and perspectives of individuals outside perceived boundaries the Legacy Leader® actively seeks to include as many as possible, wherever possible and appropriate, in the community of the whole. ■ **FROM the "darkness beyond..."** **TO enlightened communication** Instead of leaving others "in the dark" from a lack of inclusive communication, the Legacy Leader® is deliberate about bringing the whole into a complete communication loop, keeping all informed and up to date. Good and thoughtful communication is an important element of showing respect and acknowledging the potential contribution of others. ■ **FROM scattered pieces...** **TO a healthy whole** Instead of many pieces functioning independently, and often without the benefit of input or feedback from "outside" pieces, the Legacy Leadership® organization functions smoothly as an entity, with all pieces contributing to the successful operation of the whole.

Legacy Leaders® see people through a different set of lenses. They don't see labels or biases. They DON'T see "those engineers, those women, those men, those marketing people, those consultants, those HR people." What may appear to be differences are seen rather as strengths that contribute to the wholeness and success of the organization.

Critical Success Skills

4 Advocator of Differences and Community™

In order to enhance the practical application of Legacy Leadership®, each of the 5 Best Practices contains 10 Critical Success Skills. These skills contain the competencies, attitudes and behaviors which are the hallmark of great leaders. These 10 skills/ competencies are the basis of the ten assessment questions for Best Practice 4 in the Legacy Leadership® Competency Inventory (LLCI)™.

CRITICAL SUCCESS SKILLS

1. Be able to take a stand for a person, practice or cause.

2. Constantly raise visibility of individuals by mentoring/developing them.

3. Advocate for a strengths-based culture.

4. Be a connoisseur of talent, recognizing, valuing and utilizing the best each person has to offer.

5. Insist on building teams with diverse approaches and capabilities.

6. Look for/create cross-functional opportunities to develop unique talent.

7. Promote inter-departmental collaboration, rather than "silo" orientation.

8. Consider impact of actions on greater community (beyond organization).

9. Maintain ongoing dialogue/involvement with internal/external communities.

10. Promote inclusive environment to unite toward common focus.

Advocator of Differences and Community™

An ADVOCATOR stands in support of a cause, a practice or a person on its or their behalf.

Definition	**DIFFERENCES** are those qualities that distinguish people or things from other people or things.	**COMMUNITY** is a group of people with shared interest working together to achieve shared success.
What it IS: The Legacy Leader® will:	<ul><li>advocate differences by seeking relationships with team members, by discovering, acknowledging, and accepting differences in those relationships, and by promoting individual strengths and perspectives for the greater whole of the organization.</li><li>encourage, promote and protect such advocacy by drawing together individuals who contribute diverse perspectives for a greater good, and will model the endorsement and leveraging of differences into added value for the whole.</li><li>establish and maintain this advocacy so that it becomes foundational to all activities.</li></ul>	<ul><li>Advocate the promoting and combining of differences into a unified whole, and will then stand in support of this community as it builds relationships— from within and without the organization— that enlarge and expand the growth of the community, and the success of the organization.</li><li>encourage, promote, protect and advocate for this community by helping individuals and teams discover strengths in both commonality and differences that can be instrumental in the growth of the individual, the community and the organization, and by modeling an attitude of connectedness and inclusion.</li><li>maintain this advocacy of community so that it becomes foundational to all activities.</li></ul>
What it is NOT:	<ul><li>Equal Employment Opportunity</li><li>The token "oddball"</li><li>Giving "lip service"</li></ul>	<ul><li>Manipulation</li><li>"Rally 'round the flag" time</li><li>Forced inclusion</li></ul>
Factors for Success (what must be in place)	<ul><li>Acknowledgement of the importance and benefit of differences</li><li>Environment that promotes relationships</li><li>Openness to diverse perspectives</li><li>Complete lack of prejudices or other difference-limiting mindsets</li><li>Passion for learning, discovery</li><li>Individual egos that take a backseat to wholeness</li><li>Lack of labels and stereotypes</li></ul>	<ul><li>Good team-building environment</li><li>Acknowledgement that all parts needed to make the whole</li><li>Management that promotes community</li><li>Understanding of the strength afforded in differences</li><li>Keen desire to know others as people, not pawns</li><li>Understanding that as one grows and succeeds, ALL do.</li><li>Ability to unite differences into community process</li><li>Desire to embrace and incorporate diversity in all activities</li><li>Excellent, consistent, and clear communication</li></ul>
Challenges (Potential Barriers)	<ul><li>Labels and prejudices</li><li>Turf protection ("them" against "us")</li><li>Comfort zones</li><li>"Rubber stamp" or "cookie cutter" mentality</li><li>Non-inclusive belief systems</li><li>"First sight" snap judgments</li><li>Inability to see beyond appearances</li></ul>	<ul><li>Hidden, or even stated, organizational or personal agendas</li><li>Organizational or personal lack of concern for others</li><li>A need to get the "credit" for successes</li><li>Lack of respect for others</li><li>Command-and-control rather than relational environment</li><li>Inability to see the "trees" for the forest</li><li>Personal, departmental or organizational "walls"</li><li>Communication deficiencies</li></ul>
Behaviors and Competencies **The Holder of this will...**	<ul><li>promote differences and value them for the whole.</li><li>know own biases, stereotypes and labels, seek to overcome.</li><li>know how he or she is different.</li><li>discover how others see the world and individual situations.</li><li>be curious about differences, desire to learn more about them.</li><li>reframe how they think and how they approach people who are "different" from themselves.</li><li>practice active and interested listening.</li><li>recap, summarize conversation for clarity</li><li>seek common ground/good in environment of differences.</li><li>take time, have courage to go beyond comfort zone w/others.</li><li>practice being comfortable around those who previously evoked "discomfort."</li></ul>	<ul><li>always look for the strengths of individuals to add to the success of the whole.</li><li>see beyond boundaries of individuals, teams or departments.</li><li>always have the success of the whole in mind.</li><li>know about perspectives/strengths from all sources.</li><li>actively seek to lift up others, even those "outside" immediate corporate or departmental lines.</li><li>be aware of added benefits of inclusion.</li><li>help others discover/value own strengths, potential contributions.</li><li>have identified own strengths.</li><li>communicate well and often with all parts of the whole.</li><li>defend, support and speak up for their community.</li></ul>
LegacyShifts™	<ul><li>FROM "us against them" TO Esprit de corps</li><li>FROM "he doesn't have a clue" TO "what can he share?"</li><li>FROM individuals TO relationships</li></ul>	<ul><li>FROM exclusion TO inclusion</li><li>FROM the "darkness beyond" TO enlightened communication</li><li>FROM scattered pieces TO a healthy whole</li></ul>
Legacy Steps	1. Set aside your ego. 2. Discover/overcome personal biases/prejudices/stereotypes. 3. Actively seek out differences and the strengths within them. 4. Look for common ground. 4. Reframe how you think/approach "different." 5. Take time and effort to understand others. 6. Become an active and eager listener. 7. Actively seek opinions of those who may think differently, and value them. 8. Design conversations/meetings to be inclusive, then recap. 9. Remember that you don't have all the answers. 10. Discard old ideas of territorialism and self-protection.	1. CHOOSE to be inclusive. 2. Open doors, take down walls, break through any barriers. 3. Acknowledge and respect the contribution of others. 8. Help all discover strengths/potential contribution to whole. 5. Evaluate existing communication protocol/habits, work to widen circle, increase frequency and informative content. 6. Share information outside perceived department/team. 7. Discover your own unique strengths and perspectives. 8. Remember you are serving the vision of whole organization. 9. Support/defend the community as a whole, expose activities or behaviors that do not do this. 10. Be a leader who enables rather than hobbles growth.

5 Calibrator of Responsibility and Accountability™

5 Calibrator of Responsibility and Accountability™

Basic Definitions

A CALIBRATOR "sets the mark," determining the quantitative measurement of success (and acceptance).

Responsibility

RESPONSIBILITY is the ability to respond correctly to—and meet—stated expectations.

Accountability

ACCOUNTABILITY is the obligation to explain or justify conduct, conditions or circumstances.

Legacy Leadership® Definitions

The Legacy Leader® will calibrate responsibility and accountability by:

- demonstrating (and stating) standards of behavior, providing clarity about expectations of results, and by ensuring measurement of progress towards vision.

- defining those things for which all are responsible, including him or herself, and by providing a measurement system and process to evaluate the success of accomplishments and results, and celebrating accomplished goals.

- encouraging, promoting and protecting such calibration by making adjustments for new information and change, providing a consistent role model for personal accountability, standards for behavior and results, and the consistent milestone marking and evaluation of the process toward expected outcome.

- establishing and maintaining this calibration so that it becomes foundational to all activities.

Accountabilities are those things for which we are responsible, that we can be counted on to accomplish, and expected by others to do. Accountabilities have a part in individual, team, departmental and whole community process.

A "monitor" catches people breaking the rules. A CALIBRATOR models and sees consistent acceptable behavior, names it, and holds it up as a mirror for themselves and others.

5

Calibrating **RESPONSIBILITY**	*Calibrating* **ACCOUNTABILITY**
Calibrating Responsibility is NOT: ■ **Discipline** Responsibility calibrated by a Legacy Leader® is NOT discipline. Discipline involves rigid rules and external punishment. Calibration of responsibility provides guidance, direction, careful correction, consistent growth and celebration of success. ■ **Being the "Hall Monitor"** The calibrating of responsibility by Legacy Leadership® is NOT roaming the halls looking for problem children or deviant behavior. A Legacy Leader® consistently models acceptable behavior, and if necessary, states it as well; and is willing and able to change the model to fulfill commitments without compromising values and vision. ■ **A Rule Book** The calibration of responsibility by Legacy Leadership® is NOT the compilation of a book of rules and regulations, though the organization may very well have such a set of guidelines. This practice involves more on the part of the leader as a mirror of acceptable and expected behavior, and as a nurturer and promoter of personal, professional and organizational growth.	**Calibrating Accountability is NOT:** ■ **Being "called on the carpet"** Accountability calibrated by a Legacy Leader® is NOT the act of calling individual employees on the carpet to justify their work. True calibration of accountability is a standard set by leadership by which the whole community has ownership of the process—and therefore are wholly accountable for progress made during that process. ■ **Pointing fingers or playing the "blame game"** The calibration of accountability through Legacy Leadership® is NOT pointing fingers for blame and making individuals or departments scapegoats when something goes wrong. It acknowledges that the process is flawed, asks everyone to own part of that, and then seeks to learn how to grow and improve. ■ **The "end justifies the means"** Accountabilities calibrated by a Legacy Leader® are NOT a license for unacceptable behavior, or a mindset that expects results—no matter what. The end does not justify the means if vision and values are compromised. The means—the process—is the focus here. How we have conducted ourselves on the process road to the "end" is what must be justified, and kept accountable.

Critical Factors

5	*Calibrating* **RESPONSIBILITY**	*Calibrating* **ACCOUNTABILITY**
Factors for Success	■ Leaders who provide consistent role models of acceptable behavior ■ Clear expectations ■ Stated and understood vision and values ■ Desire to develop others ■ The right people in the right jobs ■ Excellent communication system ■ Measurement systems	■ Clarity ■ Modeling of personal responsibility ■ Respect for others ■ Desire to develop others ■ Clear standards of behavior, expectations and accountabilities ■ Inclusiveness ■ Process of measurement ■ Identified levels of accountability (individual, team, department, etc.) ■ Excellent, consistent, and clear communication
Challenges (Potential Barriers)	■ Leaders that do not fulfill their own responsibilities ■ Unstated or unclear expectations, vision and values ■ No process for evaluation and guidance ■ Lack of compassion and caring for people ■ Poor placement and matching of people with responsibilities ■ No understanding of calibration vs. discipline ■ No measurement systems	■ Leaders not holding self accountable ■ No standards ■ Qualifiers and exceptions to accountability ■ No roadmap ■ Lack of respect for others ■ Either/or thinking ■ Forgetting the customer ■ No measurement process ■ Communication deficiencies

RESPONSIBILITIES: What I do
ACCOUNTABILITIES: The results I produce

Application

5	*Calibrating* **RESPONSIBILITY**	*Calibrating* **ACCOUNTABILITY**
Behaviors and Competencies	**A Calibrator of Responsibility:** ■ has very clearly defined vision and values, for themselves and of the organization. ■ knows instinctively what is acceptable and "right" behavior, and also knows what is not. ■ helps insure that the right people are in the right positions within the organization. ■ knows how to celebrate the accomplishment of goals and vision. ■ makes constant comparisons to, and checks against, vision and values and other stated milestones. ■ focuses on what went right and what can be done differently, instead of what went wrong. ■ holds themselves responsible first. ■ plans for the making of adjustments in standards of behavior as a result of new information or changes, but never compromises vision and values. ■ provides a consistent role model of acceptable, expected behavior. ■ ensures measurement of progress toward the vision. ■ makes no exceptions to the expectations for responsible and acceptable behavior.	**A Calibrator of Accountability:** ■ respects others. ■ realizes that accountabilities are shared. ■ provides a consistent role model of personal accountability. ■ sets and communicates the expectations, milestones, measurement and requirements of accountabilities. ■ regularly measures accountabilities and compares against existing vision and values. ■ understands that this is a growth process, not a place for blaming. ■ must provide the tools (content, context, resources) so that a worker can learn and have all that is needed to fulfill their responsibilities, then together they are responsible and accountable for process and outcome. ■ focuses on employees, encouraging employees to focus on themselves and the customer, vendor, or other organizational vision. ■ ensures that people do those things for which they are responsible, and shares responsibility and challenges for processes and outcomes that may fall short of vision. ■ is a directional leader.

**Legacy Leaders® show others how to
seek to find a way together—
not a way out.**

Legacy Steps

5

Calibrating **RESPONSIBILITY**	*Calibrating* **ACCOUNTABILITY**
1. Be responsible, and expect the same of everyone else.	1. Hold yourself accountable at all times.
2. Observe and optimize employee performance by ensuring the right people are in the right positions.	2. Set and communicate clear standards.
3. Acknowledge all contributions and celebrate all successes.	3. Communicate community accountability—no exceptions.
4. Maintain a vigilant ongoing comparison of all behaviors to vision and values.	4. Remind others that the highest goal of accountability is to satisfy the customer, the vendor, or other target of organizational vision.
5. Inspire acceptable standards of behavior in others by providing the right role model.	5. Encourage frequent personal accountability checks.
6. Establish roadmaps and targeted milestones for measurement of progress toward vision.	6. Perform regular community process accountability sessions to evaluate the process and outcomes.
7. Dwell on the present and the future, not the past.	7. Encourage frequent and clear communication among all parts of the whole.
8. Make all perceived "failures" into opportunities and challenges.	8. Encourage relationship building among employees, but not "cliques."
9. Make appropriate adjustments to new information and changes.	9. Understand the differences between short –term and long-term performance outcomes, and be sure your understanding is communicated well.
10. Be sure all expectations and standards for acceptable behavior are clearly communicated, both through role modeling and other understandable means.	10. Work to keep the community of workers in partnership and ownership of the overall process and fully able and willing to be accountable together.
11. Make no exceptions.	

In this calibration process, the organization can suffer from "corporate in-breeding" - the failure to consider the customer in the calibration of responsibilities.

Language

5	*Calibrating* **RESPONSIBILITY**	*Calibrating* **ACCOUNTABILITY**
Statements	▪ Statements that illustrate good examples of accomplishing a task and meeting shared goals. ▪ Statements that show where learning is needed and new behaviors must be developed. ▪ Statements that congratulate everyone for responsible, professional efforts.	▪ Statements that remind all that they are in the process, and are all accountable for the results. ▪ Statements that help determine how a project or process is trackable, reportable, and explainable for future reference. ▪ Statements that consistently compare results against vision and values, and to established milestones and roadmaps.
Questions	▪ Questions that seek to determine if actions measure up to standards and levels of excellence. ▪ Questions that encourage thinking about how to meet goals and still hold to vision and values, and maintain acceptable behaviors. ▪ Questions that will determine what went right with a project, find challenges and grow from experiences.	▪ Questions that create a path to a better process with a better outcome. ▪ Questions that encourage all individual parts of the "community" to contribute their very best to the process. ▪ Questions that seek how to determine the best method of measurement of accomplishment for a project.

What went wrong is in the past, and serves no purpose other than learning. What went right adds insight, energy and value to the community.

Legacy Shifts ™

5	*Calibrating* **RESPONSIBILITY**	*Calibrating* **ACCOUNTABILITY**
(the Legacy Leader® CREATES the environment that generates these shifts)	■ **FROM what went wrong...TO how can we do it better?** Instead of focusing on the "mistakes" or failed behavior, a shift to focusing on what went right, then to how something can be accomplished in a more responsible manner allows for constructive learning and growth. ■ **FROM do your own thing...TO do the responsible thing** Instead of a wide range of varying degrees of responsibility and behaviors concerning a targeted goal, calibrated responsibility gives everyone a clear picture of what is expected, and how to perform responsibly, beginning with—and modeled by—the leader. ■ **FROM mismatched...TO perfect match** Instead of employees whose strengths and skills do not match their position, the organization practicing the calibration of responsibility actively seeks to place people in the positions where they can make the greatest contribution, utilize all the strengths they have developed, and grow the ones with potential. This calibration effort involves ongoing observation for optimization of employee skills.	■ **FROM worker...TO owner** Instead of working as a "paid employee" to do a job for someone else, the worker becomes an owner in the accountability process, sharing all challenges and giving their best to the process. Some companies have chosen to actually make their employees owners from a financial standpoint, but even without this arrangement leaders can make intellectual and emotional owners of every individual, inviting their freely given best for the benefit of the whole. This environment is created by the Legacy Leader®. ■ **FROM "it's on YOUR head..." TO it's on OUR shoulders** Instead of looking for scapegoats and "blamees" for failed process or outcome, the Legacy Leader® leads a shift to shared accountability, and shared process for achievement and success. "Who did what wrong" is not so important as "how can we do it better?" The shoulders of accountability are collective, not individual. ■ **FROM doing my job...TO celebrating our achievement** Instead of a lot of individuals just "doing their jobs," the community whole shares in the accountability as well as the celebration of process and outcome. Growth occurs on an individual as well as a community level when each part is accountable to the whole. Community accountability insures shared participation in both challenges and victories.

Critical Success Skills

5 Calibrator of Responsibility and Accountability™

In order to enhance the practical application of Legacy Leadership®, each of the 5 Best Practices contains 10 Critical Success Skills. These skills contain the competencies, attitudes and behaviors which are the hallmark of great leaders. These 10 skills/competencies are the basis of the ten assessment questions for Best Practice 5 in the Legacy Leadership® Competency Inventory (LLCI)™.

CRITICAL SUCCESS SKILLS

1. Execute strategic plan; use appropriate checks and balances to reach goals.

2. Have "finger on the pulse" of organization, know milestone status.

3. Have team members clear about position responsibilities and how they fit into direction and deliverables.

4. Require peak performance and support all with appropriate resources.

5. Provide regular feedback/coaching, take action when low performance.

6. Have clearly defined personal and organizational accountabilities.

7. Have clearly developed action plan with benchmarks, milestones and provisions for adjustments.

8. Model sense of urgency for accomplishment and response to change.

9. Be alert to trends which may affect results; recalibrate where necessary.

10. Gain commitment from team with established accountabilities, appropriate consequences/rewards.

Calibrator of Responsibility and Accountability™

A CALIBRATOR "sets the mark," determining the quantitative measurement of acceptance.

	RESPONSIBILITY is the ability to respond correctly to—and meet—stated expectations.	ACCOUNTABILITY is the obligation to explain or justify conduct, conditions or circumstances.
Definition		
What it IS: The Legacy Leader® will:	■ calibrate responsibility by demonstrating (and stating) standards of behavior, providing clarity about expectations of results, and by ensuring measurement of progress towards vision. ■ encourage, promote and protect such calibration of responsibility by adjustments for new information and change, providing a consistent role model, and by celebration of accomplished results. ■ establish and maintain this calibration so that it becomes foundational to all activities.	■ calibrate accountability by defining those things for which all are responsible, including themselves, and by providing a measurement system and process to evaluate the success of accomplishments and results. ■ encourage, promote, protect and calibrate such accountability by providing a role model for personal responsibility, standards for behavior and results and the consistent milestone marking and evaluation of the process toward expected outcome. ■ maintain this calibration of accountability so that it becomes foundational to all activities.
What it is NOT:	■ Discipline ■ Being the "Hall Monitor" ■ A Rule Book	■ Being "called on the carpet" ■ Pointing fingers or playing the "blame game" ■ The "end justifies the means"
Factors for Success (what must be in place)	■ Leaders who provide consistent role models of acceptable behavior ■ Clear expectations ■ Stated and understood vision and values ■ Desire to develop others ■ The right people in the right jobs ■ Excellent communication system ■ Measurement systems	■ Clarity ■ Modeling of personal responsibility ■ Respect for others, desire to develop others ■ Clear standards of behavior, expectations and accountabilities ■ Inclusiveness ■ Process of measurement ■ Identified levels of accountability (individual, team, dept., etc.) ■ Excellent, consistent, and clear communication
Challenges (Potential Barriers)	■ Leaders that do not fulfill their own responsibilities ■ Unstated or unclear expectations, vision and values ■ No process for evaluation and guidance ■ Lack of compassion and caring for people ■ Poor placement and matching of people with responsibilities ■ No understanding of calibration vs. discipline ■ No measurement systems	■ Leaders not holding self accountable ■ No standards, no measurement process, no roadmap ■ Qualifiers and exceptions to accountability ■ Lack of respect for others ■ Either/or thinking ■ Forgetting the customer ■ Communication deficiencies
Behaviors and Competencies **The Holder of this will...**	■ have clearly defined vision/values, for self and organization. ■ know instinctively what is acceptable/"right" behavior, or not. ■ help insure that the right people are in the right positions. ■ know how to celebrate accomplishment of goals and vision. ■ make constant comparisons to and checks against vision and values and other stated milestones. ■ focus on what went right and what can be done differently, instead of what went wrong. ■ hold themselves responsible first. ■ plan for adjustments in standards as a result of new information/changes, but never compromise vision/values. ■ provide a consistent role model of expected behavior. ■ ensure measurement of progress toward the vision. ■ make no exceptions to expectations for responsible behavior.	■ respect others. ■ realize that accountabilities are shared. ■ provide a consistent role model of personal accountability. ■ set, communicate expectations, milestones, measurement. ■ regularly measure accountabilities and compare against existing vision and values. ■ understand this is a growth process, not a place for blaming. ■ Provide tools (content, context, resources) so a worker can learn and have all that is needed to fulfill responsibilities. ■ focus on employees, ask employees to focus on themselves and customer, vendor, or other organizational vision. ■ ensure people do those things for which they are responsible, and share responsibility when outcomes fall short of vision. ■ be a directional leader.
LegacyShifts™	■ FROM "what went wrong" TO "how can we do it better" ■ FROM do your own thing TO the responsible thing ■ FROM mismatched TO perfect match	■ FROM worker TO owner ■ FROM "it's on your head" TO "it's on our shoulders" ■ FROM doing my job TO celebrating our achievement
Legacy Steps	1. Be responsible, expect the same of everyone else. 2. Observe/optimize employee performance by ensuring the right people are in the right positions. 3. Acknowledge all contributions and celebrate all successes. 4. Keep ongoing comparison of all behaviors to vision/values. 5. Inspire acceptable behavior by providing right role model. 6. Establish roadmaps and targeted milestones for measurement of progress toward vision. 7. Dwell on the present and the future, not the past. 8. Make all perceived "failures" into opportunities/challenges. 9. Make appropriate adjustments to new information/changes. 10. Be sure all expectations are clearly communicated. 11. Make no exceptions	1. Hold yourself accountable at all times. 2. Set and communicate clear standards. 3. Communicate community accountability—no exceptions. 4. Remind: highest goal of accountability to satisfy the customer, vendor, or other target of organizational vision. 5. Encourage frequent personal accountability checks. 6. Perform regular community process accountability. 7. Insure frequent/clear communication w/ all parts of whole. 8. Encourage relationship building, but not "cliques." 9. Understand differences between short-term and long-term performance outcomes. 10. Work to keep community in partnership and ownership of overall process, willing to be accountable together.

Legacy Leadership®
Development Plan

Use the input you have gained from this Field Guide, the scores obtained from your Legacy Leadership® Competency Inventory (LLCI)™ results and your own past experiences, skills and self-knowledge to write your own Development Plan for becoming a Legacy Leader®.

Development Plan: Part 1

BEST PRACTICE	Top 3 Strengths in this Best Practice	Top 3 Challenges in this Best Practice (development opportunities)	Specific skills in this Best Practice I want to develop	My goals for development of this Best Practice
Holder of Vision and Values™	1. 2. 3.	1. 2. 3.		
Creator of Collaboration and Innovation™	1. 2. 3.	1. 2. 3.		
Influencer of Inspiration and Leadership™	1. 2. 3.	1. 2. 3.		
Advocator of Differences and Community™	1. 2. 3.	1. 2. 3.		
Calibrator of Responsibility and Accountability™	1. 2. 3.	1. 2. 3.		

NOTE: The Top 3 strengths, and the Top 3 Challenges are determined from your completed Legacy Leadership® Competency Inventory (LLCI)

Continued next page...

CIRCLE THE TOP 5 AREAS YOU WISH TO DEVELOP NOW

1   Use this template to formulate a simple development plan for change, based on your answers to Part 1 of the Development Plan

2 LEADER SHIFTS		**3** Observable and Measurable **DIFFERENCES** (What will you see)
FROM ➡	**TO**	
List the top 5 areas you want to work on now in the FROM column in language that states your current behavior. List these behaviors again in the TO column to show the shift you will make. These are goal statements.		When you reach the desired state, what changes will you (and others) be able to observe and measure in these 5 areas?

ACTION ITEMS (Making it happen)	**7** **RESULTS** (Impact on you and others)
4 How will you bring about the desired shift and growth?	What do you see as the impact of making these changes? On yourself? On others? On your business? On your organization?
5 What resources do you need for this plan to succeed?	
6 When do you expect to achieve your goals?	

Development Plan: Part 3

Important Questions

If I were making a "to do" list for my personal leadership development as a Legacy Leader®, what are my **top three** commitments to myself?

1.

2.

3.

With whom will I share my Action/Development Plan and when?

How will I know when I am a Legacy Leader®? What will success look like?

If the fundamental premise of a Legacy Leader® is to teach others to be Legacy Leaders®, then: What opportunities are available to me right now to teach LL to others?

What LL supporting materials and techniques will I use to grow other leaders?

Which leaders in my organization/practice/workplace/other will I grow as Legacy Leaders® in the next four month? Year? Beyond?

Notes

Page 216

Competency Inventory

LEGACY
Leadership

NAME:

ISBN #0-9672175-4-7

Welcome to Legacy Leadership®

Now, like no other time in history, there is a need to develop strong leadership abilities. Using a model with proven success for both the best of times and worst of times, Legacy Leadership® embodies a compelling and comprehensive set of competencies and skills. Legacy Leaders® lead the way for others to follow to the edge of current development and beyond. We welcome you to Legacy Leadership®!

What Is Legacy Leadership®?

We hear stories every day about the lack of strong leadership talent. Legacy Leadership® is a comprehensive model for developing such talented leaders. It includes competencies and practices with immediate applicability to most every possibility and challenge the leader today faces. These practices embrace both vision and accountability for results, as well as methods for creating an environment for team success, strong and dependable relationships, and maximizing the talents of diverse perspectives and strengths.

Many organizations have a set of competencies with which to measure their leader performance, others do not. In either case, Legacy Leadership® provides a sound structure for such competencies to reside. With the structural map of the 5 Best Practices, you have a full and complete picture of the destination your leader development program will go, for you personally, and for those you lead. The basic focus of Legacy Leadership® is on OTHERS, rather than on the leader, in order to develop leaders who then develop other leaders. The outcome is fully developed leaders, both current and emerging, and a greatly enhanced leadership potential within the organization.

Legacy, in this model, is not about building things, but building people. It is about investing in individual leaders who then share what they have learned with others. Legacy is seen in this perpetuating cycle of leadership development that enables your personal and organizational plan to come alive and thrive. Your best self is offered to others to develop their best selves and so on, leaving a multi-generational imprint—a living legacy.

Leadership Competencies and Critical Success Skills—
The 5 Best Practices of Legacy Leadership®

Given that leadership is so complex, we have distinguished five core competency platforms and associated critical success skills for successful leadership. These platforms represent a complete set of observable and measurable behaviors. These behaviors, when used in total, are leverage points for success. We have included those practices of leadership that are essential for every leader, regardless of their industry or level within the organization.

These 5 Best Practice platforms are the context of the Legacy Leadership model, and are presented on the following page.

Continued next page...

These 5 Best Practice platforms are the context of the Legacy Leadership® model, and are presented on the following page. For each of the 5 Best Practices (competencies) there are 10 critical success skills detailed in this inventory. You will be evaluating your current skill level by responding to the 50 statements, both regarding your PERFORMANCE and the EXPECTATIONS of performance for your position. Plotting your results on the Master Scoring Grid gives you a quick glance at what you are doing well and where you can lead better.

By completing this inventory you will be learning and growing yourself as a more effective leader. Some of the statements you see here will be unfamiliar to you at first, but as you build the skills listed, your leadership will become more effective. By modeling dedication to your own development, you will set the pace for others to constantly raise levels of excellence.

There are many leaders in our world, but only those who desire to grow their competencies will be the most successful, influential and effective leaders; and more importantly, leaders whom people want and desire to follow—Legacy Leaders.

We invite you to explore your leadership capabilities and competencies based on this inventory. Build on what is working best for you, as well as what could work even better.

The 5 Best Practices

DEFINITIONS			EXPLANATION

1 Holder of Vision and Values™

HOLDER	VISION	VALUES	This Best Practice is about direction and commitment. The term "holder" indicates that the leader lives the vision and values while measuring every action against both. The leader then provides consistent focus and direction. The critical success skills include: integration of vision/values into all responsibilities, having a well-defined strategic plan, team translation of vision and values, establishing milestones and benchmarks, modeling the practice, developing the potential of others to pull out the best in them, and effectively communicating and sustaining organizational vision/values.
One who "keeps" in hand those things that are important, by embracing and encouraging their remembrance.	A clear view and understanding of realizable goals, plans and intentions.	Those things considered right, worthwhile and desirable—the basis of guiding principles and standards.	

2 Creator of Collaboration and Innovation™

CREATOR	COLLABORATION	INNOVATION	This Best Practice is about creating a positive environment for working relationships. The term "creator" indicates the leader's ability to create a learning trusting environment where collaboration and innovation can occur. The critical success skills include abilities to: unleash innovation, listen masterfully, learn from others, be aware of the bigger picture, discern when change needs to occur, and being a masterful facilitator.
One who causes something to "come into being" through original or inventive means.	The process of working together to achieve common goals instead of personal agenda.	The introduction of something new and different to the process of achieving goals	

3 Influencer of Inspiration and Leadership™

INFLUENCER	INSPIRATION	LEADERSHIP	This Best Practice is about making connections with individuals—the heart of relationships as well as leadership. The term "influencer" indicates the leader's ability to influence and inspire for positive relationships. The critical success skills include abilities to: influence positively, demonstrate high levels of emotional intelligence, bring out the best in people by developing them fully, focus on others rather than self, make tough decisions with minimal people impact, and be humble while holding resolve to accomplish stated goals.
One who brings about a desired effect in others, by direct or indirect means.	The process of animating, motivating or encouraging others to reach new levels of achievement.	The process of guiding and directing others to shared success.	

4 Advocator of Differences and Community™

ADVOCATOR	DIFFERENCES	COMMUNITY	This Best Practice is about distinguishing individual strengths and inclusion of differing perspectives. The term "advocator" indicates the leader's ability to support and stand for strengths-based talent. The critical success skills include abilities to: be an advocate of individuals, be a connoisseur of talent, insist on teams with diverse perspectives and abilities, stand for cross-functional development and collaboration, recognize community impact, and promote an inclusive environment united toward a common focus.
One who stands in support of a cause, a practice or a person on its or their behalf.	Those qualities that distinguish people or things from other people or things.	A group of people with shared interest working together to achieve shared success.	

5 Calibrator of Responsibility and Accountability™

CALIBRATOR	RESPONSIBILITY	ACCOUNTABILITY	This Best Practice is about execution and performance measured against vision and values. The term "calibrator" indicates constant vigilance, with possible adjustments, of progress toward accomplishing responsibilities and accountabilities. The critical success skills include abilities to: execute successfully, maintain a "finger on the pulse" for status measurement, require peak performance, provide feedback and coaching, have clearly defined action plans, model a sense of urgency in getting things done and respond to change, be alert to trends, and gain commitment to follow-through.
One who "sets the mark" for the quantitative measurement of success/ acceptance.	The ability to respond correctly to—and meet—stated expectations.	The obligation to justify conduct, conditions or circumstances.	

Using the Inventory

This competency inventory is an opportunity for leaders to receive information about their level of competency in each of the five practice contexts of Legacy Leadership. It provides a direction for learning, a guide for leader development and a model for developing leadership fully.

Instructions for Completion

For each Best Practice there is a set of ten descriptive statements. YOU ARE ASKED TO PROVIDE A RATING FOR **TWO QUESTIONS** FOR EACH STATEMENT:

PERFORMANCE: How often **do I exhibit** this stated behavior/attitude?
EXPECTATIONS: How often is this stated behavior/attitude **expected to occur** in my position?

Read each statement carefully, and honestly rate yourself on a scale of 1 to 5 as follows:
This statement describes my behavior/attitude (PERFORMANCE COLUMN):
The statement describes how often this behavior/attitude should occur (EXPECTATIONS):
> 1—Not At All
> 2—Occasionally
> 3—On Average
> 4—Frequently
> 5—Consistently

Rate yourself for BOTH Performance and Expectations using this scale. Answer all ten questions in each Best Practice, for a total of 50 questions, two responses (ratings) each question.

After you have rated each statement, total each column under each of the two sets of responses (Performance and Expectations) and place the added score for each of the five columns in the blanks provided. Then add the column score total across from left to right for a total score for each set of ratings on each Best Practice. Graph your responses on each page. *See the sample page following.*

Complete the Master Scoring Grid.

Next Steps: Legacy Leader® Development Plan

After you have established your baseline as a starting point, you will be able to design a leader development plan including those areas you wish to upgrade your level of performance. See page 14 for a suggested format for your plan. Work with your coach and/or leader to carry out the plan and leverage the results.

Best Practice 1: Holder of Vision and Values™

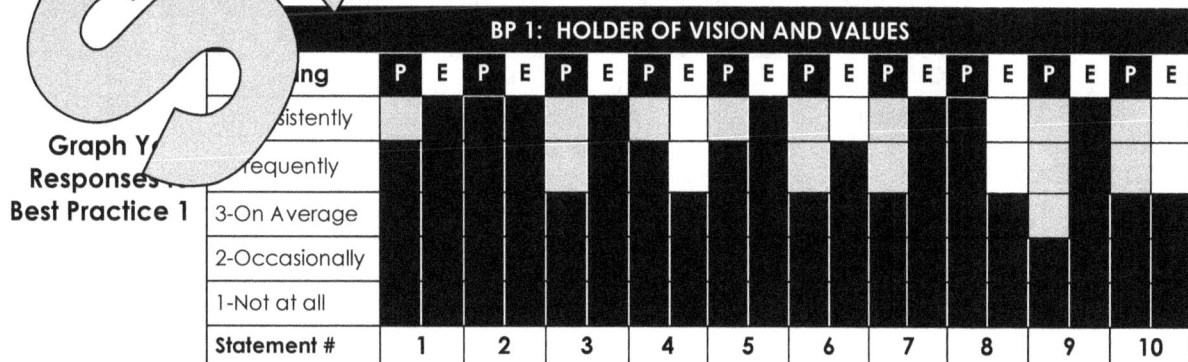

1 Rate yourself ON THIS BEST PRACTICE, using the following table. Circle one rating from EACH of the rating columns (Performance and Expectations). The ratings in the **PERFORMANCE** columns should reflect how often the stated behavior **DOES occur** with you. The ratings in the EXPECTATION columns should reflect how often each behavior **SHOULD** occur. Total each column, then add for a grand total for each set of ratings. Graph your responses below.

#	Behavior/Attitude (As it applies to this BP)	Description	Performance — Consistently 5	Frequently 4	On Average 3	Occasionally 2	Not At All 1		Expectations — Consistently 5	Frequently 4	On Average 3	Occasionally 2	Not At All 1
1	Reinforce Vision/Values	I consistently reinforce the organization's vision and values.	5	(4)	3	2	1		(5)	4	3	2	1
2	Model Principles	I intentionally model the organization's principles in everything I do with all staff.	5		3	2	1		(5)	4	3	2	1
3	Integrate Vision	I have integrated the organization's vision into my responsibilities.	5	4	(3)	2	1		(5)	4	3	2	1
4	Strategic Plan	I have a well-defined strategic plan for accomplishing the goals of the vision.	5	(4)	3	2	1		5	4	(3)	2	1
5	Team Alignment	My team has translated its daily responsibilities with the goals of the organization.	5	(4)	3	2	1		(5)	4	3	2	1
6	Established Measureables	I have established measurable benchmarks aligned with the vision.	5	4	(3)	2	1		5	(4)	3	2	1
7	Values Integration	I ensure that our values are integrated into how we do business.	5	4	(3)	2	1		(5)	4	3	2	1
8	Personal Values	I have clearly identified personal values, and "walk my talk."	(5)	4	3	2	1		5	4	(3)	2	1
9	Develop Others	It is important to develop the potential of others in the organization.	5	4	3	(2)	1		(5)	4	3	2	1
10	Communicate, Sustain Processes	I effectively communicate and sustain processes and systems to achieve organizational vision throughout my business area.	5	4	(3)	2	1		5	4	(3)	2	1
		COLUMN TOTALS	10	12	12	2	0		30	4	9	0	0
		GRAND TOTAL	36						43				

Center column note: Choose One Rating in Each Column (Performance AND Ex-)

Complete by filling in the appropriate boxes for each of the 10 statements above, FOR EACH OF THE TWO CATEGORIES: PERFORMANCE (P) AND EXPECTATION (E), so you create a bar graph to easily spot your highest and lowest ratings). (For example, if you scored a 5 on statement #1, color in all five boxes for that number.)

BP 1: HOLDER OF VISION AND VALUES

Rating	P	E	P	E	P	E	P	E	P	E	P	E	P	E	P	E	P	E	P	E
Consistently																				
Frequently																				
3-On Average																				
2-Occasionally																				
1-Not at all																				
Statement #	1		2		3		4		5		6		7		8		9		10	

Graph Your Responses for Best Practice 1

Best Practice 1: *Holder of Vision and Values*™

1 Rate yourself ON THIS BEST PRACTICE, using the following table. Circle one rating from EACH of the rating columns (Performance and Expectations). The ratings in the **PERFORMANCE** columns should reflect how often the stated behavior **DOES occur** with you. The ratings in the EXPECTATION columns should reflect how often each behavior **SHOULD** occur. Total each column, then add for a grand total for each set of ratings. Graph your responses below.

#	Behavior/ Attitude (As it applies to this BP)	Description	Performance						Expectations				
			Consistently 5	Frequently 4	On Average 3	Occasionally 2	Not At All 1	Choose One Rating in Each Column (Performance AND Expectations)	Consistently 5	Frequently 4	On Average 3	Occasionally 2	Not At All 1
1	Reinforce Vision/Values	I consistently reinforce the organization's vision and values.	5	4	3	2	1		5	4	3	2	1
2	Model Principles	I intentionally model the organization's guiding principles in everything I do with all stakeholders.	5	4	3	2	1		5	4	3	2	1
3	Integrate Vision	I have integrated the organization's vision into all of my responsibilities.	5	4	3	2	1		5	4	3	2	1
4	Strategic Plan	I have a well-defined strategic plan for accomplishing the goals of the vision.	5	4	3	2	1		5	4	3	2	1
5	Team Alignment	My team has translated and aligned its daily responsibilities with the goals of the organization.	5	4	3	2	1		5	4	3	2	1
6	Established Measureables	I have established measurable milestones and benchmarks congruent with the vision.	5	4	3	2	1		5	4	3	2	1
7	Values Integration	I ensure that organizational values are integrated into how we do business.	5	4	3	2	1		5	4	3	2	1
8	Personal Values	I have clearly identified personal values, and "walk my talk" in everything I do.	5	4	3	2	1		5	4	3	2	1
9	Develop Others	It is very important to me that I develop the potential of others in the organization.	5	4	3	2	1		5	4	3	2	1
10	Communicate, Sustain Processes	I effectively communicate and sustain processes and systems to achieve the organizational vision and values throughout my business area.	5	4	3	2	1		5	4	3	2	1
		COLUMN TOTALS											
		➡ **GRAND TOTAL**											

Completely color in the appropriate boxes for each of the 10 statements above, FOR EACH OF THE TWO CATEGORIES: PERFORMANCE (P) AND EXPECTATION (E), so you create a bar graph to easily spot your highest and lowest ratings). (For example, if you scored "5" on statement #1, color in all five boxes for that number.)

Graph Your Responses to Best Practice 1

BP 1: HOLDER OF VISION AND VALUES™																				
Rating	P	E	P	E	P	E	P	E	P	E	P	E	P	E	P	E	P	E	P	E
5-Consistently																				
4-Frequently																				
3-On Average																				
2-Occasionally																				
1-Not at all																				
Statement #	1		2		3		4		5		6		7		8		9		10	

2

Rate yourself ON THIS BEST PRACTICE, using the following table. Circle one rating from EACH of the rating columns (Performance and Expectations). The ratings in the **PERFORMANCE** columns should reflect how often the stated behavior **DOES occur** with you. The ratings in the EXPECTATION columns should reflect how often each behavior **SHOULD** occur. Total each column, then add for a grand total for each set of ratings. Graph your responses below.

#	Behavior/ Attitude (As it applies to this BP)	Description	Performance					Choose One Rating in Each Column (Performance AND Expectations)	Expectations				
			Consistently 5	Frequently 4	On Average 3	Occasionally 2	Not At All 1		Consistently 5	Frequently 4	On Average 3	Occasionally 2	Not At All 1
1	Innovative Possibilities	I create possibilities that are both innovative and sound for the organization.	5	4	3	2	1		5	4	3	2	1
2	Trusting Environment	I foster a learning, trusting environment where true collaboration and innovation are unleashed.	5	4	3	2	1		5	4	3	2	1
3	Masterful Listener	I am a masterful listener for both what is said and what is not said.	5	4	3	2	1		5	4	3	2	1
4	Comfortable Learning from	I am comfortable not knowing "the answers" and learning from individual perspectives.	5	4	3	2	1		5	4	3	2	1
5	Opportunities in Disagreement	I draw out differing perspectives and believe that disagreement is a learning opportunity.	5	4	3	2	1		5	4	3	2	1
6	Timely Questioning	I keep in mind the bigger picture while asking timely, tough questions.	5	4	3	2	1		5	4	3	2	1
7	Innovate for Future	I set the tone for thinking beyond where we are presently in order to innovate now for the future.	5	4	3	2	1		5	4	3	2	1
8	Organizational, Marketplace Projection	I can project how ideas may play out in the organization and marketplace.	5	4	3	2	1		5	4	3	2	1
9	Discern need (or not) for Change	I can discern, and assist others to understand, when change needs to occur and when it does not.	5	4	3	2	1		5	4	3	2	1
10	Facilitate Best Group Thinking	I am a masterful facilitator of conversations such that everyone contributes their best thinking toward the task/issue at hand.	5	4	3	2	1		5	4	3	2	1
		COLUMN TOTALS											
		➡ **GRAND TOTAL**											

Completely color in the appropriate boxes for each of the 10 statements above, FOR EACH OF THE TWO CATEGORIES: PERFORMANCE (P) AND EXPECTATION (E), so you create a bar graph to easily spot your highest and lowest ratings). (For example, if you scored "5" on statement #1, color in all five boxes for that number.)

Graph Your Responses to Best Practice 2

BP 2: CREATOR OF COLLABORATION AND INNOVATION™																				
Rating	P	E	P	E	P	E	P	E	P	E	P	E	P	E	P	E	P	E	P	E
5-Consistently																				
4-Frequently																				
3-On Average																				
2-Occasionally																				
1-Not at all																				
Statement #	1		2		3		4		5		6		7		8		9		10	

3

Rate yourself ON THIS BEST PRACTICE, using the following table. Circle one rating from EACH of the rating columns (Performance and Expectations). The ratings in the **PERFORMANCE** columns should reflect how often the stated behavior **DOES occur** with you. The ratings in the EXPECTATION columns should reflect how often each behavior **SHOULD** occur. Total each column, then add for a grand total for each set of ratings. Graph your responses below.

#	Behavior/ Attitude (As it applies to this BP)	Description	Performance					Choose One Rating in Each Column (Performance AND Expectations)	Expectations				
			Consistently 5	*Frequently* 4	*On Average* 3	*Occasionally* 2	*Not At All* 1		*Consistently* 5	*Frequently* 4	*On Average* 3	*Occasionally* 2	*Not At All* 1
1	Develop Relationships	I am very adept at developing and maintaining relationships.	5	4	3	2	1		5	4	3	2	1
2	Energy to Influence	I use my emotional intelligence and positive energy to influence others.	5	4	3	2	1		5	4	3	2	1
3	Model Positive Perspective	I choose to model the positive perspective in all situations.	5	4	3	2	1		5	4	3	2	1
4	Evoke Best in Others	I bring out the best in people.	5	4	3	2	1		5	4	3	2	1
5	Acknowledge Contributions	I constantly acknowledge and recognize the attributes and contributions of others.	5	4	3	2	1		5	4	3	2	1
6	Delegate for Development	I intentionally delegate for the development of others.	5	4	3	2	1		5	4	3	2	1
7	Showcase Others	I lead with a constant focus on showcasing others rather than myself.	5	4	3	2	1		5	4	3	2	1
8	Inspiring Risk Taker	I have the ability and courage to take risks and inspire others to follow.	5	4	3	2	1		5	4	3	2	1
9	Minimize Negative	I am able to make tough decisions that have minimal negative impact.	5	4	3	2	1		5	4	3	2	1
10	Meet goals thru Others/Humility, Resolve	I lead with humility and fierce resolve to accomplish the goals of the organization through others.	5	4	3	2	1		5	4	3	2	1
		COLUMN TOTALS											
		➡ **GRAND TOTAL**											

Completely color in the appropriate boxes for each of the 10 statements above, FOR EACH OF THE TWO CATEGORIES: PERFORMANCE (P) AND EXPECTATION (E), so you create a bar graph to easily spot your highest and lowest ratings). (For example, if you scored "5" on statement #1, color in all five boxes for that number.)

Graph Your Responses to Best Practice 3

BP 3: INFLUENCER OF INSPIRATION AND LEADERSHIP™																				
Rating	P	E	P	E	P	E	P	E	P	E	P	E	P	E	P	E	P	E	P	E
5-Consistently																				
4-Frequently																				
3-On Average																				
2-Occasionally																				
1-Not at all																				
Statement #	1		2		3		4		5		6		7		8		9		10	

4

Rate yourself ON THIS BEST PRACTICE, using the following table. Circle one rating from EACH of the rating columns (Performance and Expectations). The ratings in the **PERFORMANCE** columns should reflect how often the stated behavior **DOES occur** with you. The ratings in the EXPECTATION columns should reflect how often each behavior **SHOULD** occur. Total each column, then add for a grand total for each set of ratings. Graph your responses below.

#	Behavior/ Attitude (As it applies to this BP)	Description	Performance Consistently 5	Frequently 4	On Average 3	Occasionally 2	Not At All 1	Choose One Rating in Each Column (Performance AND Expectations)	Expectations Consistently 5	Frequently 4	On Average 3	Occasionally 2	Not At All 1
1	Ready Advocate	I am able to take a stand for a person, practice, or cause.	5	4	3	2	1		5	4	3	2	1
2	Mentor for Visibility	I constantly raise the visibility of individuals by mentoring and developing them.	5	4	3	2	1		5	4	3	2	1
3	Strengths-Based Culture	I am an advocate for a strengths-based culture where everyone works from their strengths.	5	4	3	2	1		5	4	3	2	1
4	Connoisseur of Talent	I am a connoisseur of talent, recognizing, valuing and utilizing the best each person has to offer.	5	4	3	2	1		5	4	3	2	1
5	Team Diversity	I insist on having teams of individuals with diverse approaches and capabilities.	5	4	3	2	1		5	4	3	2	1
6	Cross-Functional Opportunities	I look for cross-functional opportunities where unique talent can be developed.	5	4	3	2	1		5	4	3	2	1
7	Inter-Department Collaboration	I promote inter-departmental collaboration rather than "silo" orientation.	5	4	3	2	1		5	4	3	2	1
8	Consider Greater Community	I consider the impact of actions on the greater community beyond organizational boundaries.	5	4	3	2	1		5	4	3	2	1
9	Internal-External Communication	I have ongoing dialogue and involvement with internal and external communities.	5	4	3	2	1		5	4	3	2	1
10	United Inclusive Environment	I promote an inclusive environment that unites towards a common focus.	5	4	3	2	1		5	4	3	2	1
		COLUMN TOTALS											
		➡ **GRAND TOTAL**											

Completely color in the appropriate boxes for each of the 10 statements above, FOR EACH OF THE TWO CATEGORIES: PERFORMANCE (P) AND EXPECTATION (E), so you create a bar graph to easily spot your highest and lowest ratings). (For example, if you scored "5" on statement #1, color in all five boxes for that number.)

	BP 4: ADVOCATOR OF DIFFERENCES AND COMMUNITY™																				
	Rating	P	E	P	E	P	E	P	E	P	E	P	E	P	E	P	E	P	E	P	E
Graph Your Responses to Best Practice 4	5-Consistently																				
	4-Frequently																				
	3-On Average																				
	2-Occasionally																				
	1-Not at all																				
	Statement #	1		2		3		4		5		6		7		8		9		10	

Best Practice 5: *Calibrator of Responsibility and Accountability*™

5

Rate yourself ON THIS BEST PRACTICE, using the following table. Circle one rating from EACH of the rating columns (Performance and Expectations). The ratings in the **PERFORMANCE** columns should reflect how often the stated behavior **DOES occur** with you. The ratings in the EXPECTATION columns should reflect how often each behavior **SHOULD** occur. Total each column, then add for a grand total for each set of ratings. Graph your responses below.

#	Behavior/ Attitude (As it applies to this BP)	Description	Performance Consistently 5	Frequently 4	On Average 3	Occasionally 2	Not At All 1	Choose One Rating in Each Column (Performance AND Expectations)	Expectations Consistently 5	Frequently 4	On Average 3	Occasionally 2	Not At All 1
1	Strategic Plan with Checks and Balances	I execute the organization's strategic plan and use appropriate checks and balances to reach the goals.	5	4	3	2	1		5	4	3	2	1
2	Know Milestone Status	I have my "finger on the pulse" of the organization and know our milestone status.	5	4	3	2	1		5	4	3	2	1
3	Team Members Clear about Responsibilities	Individuals in my team are clear about position responsibilities and how they fit into the organization's direction and deliverables.	5	4	3	2	1		5	4	3	2	1
4	Require Peak Performance/	I require peak performance and support everyone with appropriate resources.	5	4	3	2	1		5	4	3	2	1
5	Feedback and Appropriate Action	I provide regular feedback and coaching, and take action when performance does not meet stated expectations.	5	4	3	2	1		5	4	3	2	1
6	Personal, Organizational	I have clearly defined accountabilities for myself and my organization.	5	4	3	2	1		5	4	3	2	1
7	Action Plan, Provision for Adjustments	I have a clearly developed action plan with benchmarks and milestones, and provisions for making adjustments along the way.	5	4	3	2	1		5	4	3	2	1
8	Urgency in Achievement	I model a sense of urgency both in getting things done and responding to change.	5	4	3	2	1		5	4	3	2	1
9	Alert to Trends, Recalibrates	I am alert to trends that potentially affect results, and re-calibrate action plans where necessary.	5	4	3	2	1		5	4	3	2	1
10	Team Commitment, Appropriate Consequences	I have gained commitment from everyone in my area of responsibility, and have established accountabilities with appropriate consequences and rewards.	5	4	3	2	1		5	4	3	2	1
		COLUMN TOTALS											
		➡ **GRAND TOTAL**											

Completely color in the appropriate boxes for each of the 10 statements above, FOR EACH OF THE TWO CATEGORIES: PERFORMANCE (P) AND EXPECTATION (E), so you create a bar graph to easily spot your highest and lowest ratings). (For example, if you scored "5" on statement #1, color in all five boxes for that number.)

Graph Your Responses to Best Practice 5

BP 5: CALIBRATOR OF RESPONSIBILITY AND ACCOUNTABILITY™																				
Rating	P	E	P	E	P	E	P	E	P	E	P	E	P	E	P	E	P	E	P	E
5-Consistently																				
4-Frequently																				
3-On Average																				
2-Occasionally																				
1-Not at all																				
Statement #	1		2		3		4		5		6		7		8		9		10	

Master Scoring Grid

Transfer the total scores from each Best Practice page.

<table>
<tr>
<th rowspan="4">TOTAL SCORES And LEVELS</th>
<th colspan="10">Best Practice</th>
</tr>
<tr>
<th colspan="2">1
Holder of Vision and Values™</th>
<th colspan="2">2
Creator of Collaboration and Innovation™</th>
<th colspan="2">3
Influencer of Inspiration and Leadership™</th>
<th colspan="2">4
Advocator of Differences and Community™</th>
<th colspan="2">5
Calibrator of Responsibility and Accountability™</th>
</tr>
<tr>
<th>P</th><th>E</th><th>P</th><th>E</th><th>P</th><th>E</th><th>P</th><th>E</th><th>P</th><th>E</th>
</tr>
<tr>
<th>Performance</th><th>Expectation</th><th>Performance</th><th>Expectation</th><th>Performance</th><th>Expectation</th><th>Performance</th><th>Expectation</th><th>Performance</th><th>Expectation</th>
</tr>
<tr>
<td>Practice Mastery</td>
<td>46-50</td><td>46-50</td><td>46-50</td><td>46-50</td><td>46-50</td><td>46-50</td><td>46-50</td><td>46-50</td><td>46-50</td><td>46-50</td>
</tr>
<tr>
<td>Practice Proficiency</td>
<td>40-45</td><td>40-45</td><td>40-45</td><td>40-45</td><td>40-45</td><td>40-45</td><td>40-45</td><td>40-45</td><td>40-45</td><td>40-45</td>
</tr>
<tr>
<td>Practice Apprenticeship</td>
<td>25-39</td><td>25-39</td><td>25-39</td><td>25-39</td><td>25-39</td><td>25-39</td><td>25-39</td><td>25-39</td><td>25-39</td><td>25-39</td>
</tr>
<tr>
<td>Practice Knowledge</td>
<td>16-24</td><td>16-24</td><td>16-24</td><td>16-24</td><td>16-24</td><td>16-24</td><td>16-24</td><td>16-24</td><td>16-24</td><td>16-24</td>
</tr>
<tr>
<td>Practice Awareness</td>
<td>10-15</td><td>10-15</td><td>10-15</td><td>10-15</td><td>10-15</td><td>10-15</td><td>10-15</td><td>10-15</td><td>10-15</td><td>10-15</td>
</tr>
</table>

Leadership Development Plan

Use this page to commit in writing your plan for development. Work with your coach to carry out the plan and leverage the results. Use the following pages for more room to write, if needed.

A – KEY PARTICIPANTS
(Name those individuals who will be most involved in helping you track success and holding you accountable.)

Name:

    Coach:

    Others:

B – BEST PRACTICE DEVELOPMENT AREAS

Competency Areas:	Other(s):
(List the one or two Best Practices in which development is a priority.)	*(List the skills from the LLCI that you want to work on specifically.)*

C - GOALS
(Develop a goal statement that includes exactly what you want to accomplish for each area you are developing.)

D – BEHAVIOR CHANGES
(What new behavior will you and others be observing as you are successful in these development areas?)

E - MEASURABLES
(How will you measure these successes?)

F - IMPACT
(What do you see as the impact of making these changes? On self? On others? On your business? On your organization?)

Notes

Page 231

CoachWorks®
The **LEGACY** Leader® Company

Who Is CoachWorks?

As pioneers and leaders in the Executive Coaching profession, CoachWorks® coaches are uniquely positioned to work with leaders who want to accelerate their effectiveness and sustain organizational vitality. Our mission is to create, inspire and coach *LegacyLeaders*® who in turn are transforming their sphere of influence and creating legacy communities with stakeholders who achieve their best.

Founded in 1995, CoachWorks® International is an acclaimed worldwide provider of leadership development services. Its coaches are thought leaders in the profession of executive coaching. They coach key leaders through change implementation until the change becomes the sustainable new way of working.

Development Methodology for the
Legacy Leadership® Competency Inventory (LLCI)™

The LLCI was developed by Dr. Lee Smith and Dr. Jeannine Sandstrom, based on twenty years of observation and experience with leaders, leadership programs and the use of other models. In working with hundreds of leaders, behavioral indicators for successful leadership practices were identified. Over time, more than 150 leadership skill sets were reduced to the 50 critical success skills that support the definition of Legacy Leadership. Data was collected on the norms for the scoring grid, as well as the variable factors on the scale. Background validity included review of research and statistics about leadership, review of practices, extrapolation from the statistics and anecdotal evidence in the leadership literature, as well as our own work. Face validity in the use of the LLCI has been, and continues to be, supported by ongoing collection of data.

The Legacy Leadership® Competency Inventory (LLCI)™ is also available online as a tool 360 Feedback Tool for personal or corporate use. Contact CoachWorks® International for more information.

For More Information Contact: